NESS BOSCH

Sacred Bones Magic Bones

STORIES FROM THE PATH OF THE BONES

of antiquity, Ness Bosch writes in a relatable and informative way, offering practical guidance and endless inspiration for the aspiring bone-worker.

Vikki Bramshaw, author of *Dionysos: Exciter to Frenzy* and *New Forest Folklore, Traditions & Charms*

Ness Bosch's *Sacred Bones, Magic Bones* is a wonderful overview of the magical history — and present — of the most immediately tangible portals to spirit that we have: our bones. Featuring stories of bones from across various times and cultures, this book offers insight into the significant role that human and animal bones have played throughout the course of human spirituality. Bosch awakens the reader's awareness to the omnipresence of ancestral memory which reverberates within our very skeletons. Such spiritual memory and power are also held, of course, within the skeletal remains animals and shells lying upon the beach. This knowledge is brought to life through Bosch's provision of stories, fascinating personal anecdotes, and unique spell suggestions. *Sacred Bones, Magic Bones* is a resource that guides and reminds the reader of the inter-connectedness of us all, of all people and creatures upon this earth, past, present, and future.

Olivia Church, author of *Isis: Great of Magic, She of 10,000 Names* and *Sekhmet: Lady of Flame, Eye of Ra*

Ness Bosch's book *Sacred Bones, Magic Bones* brings us back to one of the most ancient forms of magic and witchcraft. Bosch binds together lore, history, and magical uses of the bones that connect us to the ancestors so that we may summon the primal forces of the past to secure our future. This book is recommended for anyone seeking to learn the mysteries of bone magic.

Chris Allaun, author of *A Guide of Spirits: The Psychopomp's Manual for Transitioning the Dead into the Afterlife*

Sacred Bones, Magic Bones

Ness Bosch

Honouring with this book my blood and bones,
those who came before me, my ancestors,
and honouring those who came from me.
To my children, Kiran Alexander,
Lenora Sophia and Duncan Orion.

Sacred Bones, Magic Bones

Stories from the Path of the Bones

Ness Bosch

**MOON
BOOKS**

Winchester, UK
Washington, USA

JOHN HUNT PUBLISHING

First published by Moon Books, 2024
Moon Books is an imprint of John Hunt Publishing Ltd., No. 3 East Street, Alresford
Hampshire SO24 9EE, UK
office@jhpbooks.net
www.johnhuntpublishing.com
www.moon-books.net

For distributor details and how to order please visit the 'Ordering' section on our website.

Text copyright: Ness Bosch 2023

ISBN: 978 1 80341 212 2
978 1 80341 213 9 (ebook)
Library of Congress Control Number: 2023932248

A CIP catalogue record for this book is available from the British Library.

Design: Lapiz Digital Services

UK: Printed and bound by CPI Group (UK) Ltd, Croydon, CR0 4YY
Printed in North America by CPI GPS partners

We operate a distinctive and ethical publishing philosophy in
all areas of our business, from our global network of authors to
production and worldwide distribution.

Contents

Disclaimer

The information given as part of this book is strictly for educational and entertainment purposes. In absolutely no way is it meant as a substitute for proper medical diagnosis and treatment by registered healthcare professionals. It is very strongly recommended that you consult a licensed healthcare practitioner for any physical or psychological ailments you may have.

Acknowledgements

I would like to start by naming people who, in one way or another, have influenced my path:

My Grandparents, Jose Ruiz "El Lucio", Gracia Cañizarez and my Great-grandmother Fefa. For being my medicine, my freedom and my refuge in the mountains. My father Juan Bosch Cueto, for the books, the sea, the stories, the trips and the scars that helped me open bridges to the invisible worlds, to find my magic, my shadow and my strength. Also, not to fear the immensity of the world or the human soul. To my very large family in general. My mother, for she was my connection to the mountains, to my sister Raquel, and my brother Ulises, our particular Odysseus sailing the seven seas. To the Bosch Clan for all the adventures of my childhood and the music. To my Aunt Mili for always being my shield within the Bosch Clan and believing in me. To my Uncle Manolo for always being there. To my friend, Pepe, for the same reason. To Bobby Longman, Cai, to Lourdes, Luis Caldery, Martin, Haydee, et mon cher soul sister, Sophie Nusslé, and her family, for always being there and being the best Madrina my children could have. Thank you to everyone who helped me believe in my magic and medicine and so many other things. To Yidina, Shivani and Stephen my Frog Friends, to Sorita, Lesley, Morgana, Carmen, Nirva, Naomi, J. Stella Maris, Garry, Louise, Sol, Melissa, Amalia, Mati, Estrella and the friends, teachers and students I met walking the spiritual path. To my friends in Spain for the laughter and affection: Loli and family, Mariola, Dufi, Ino, Loreto, Luisa, Cristina, Reyes, Judith, Minerva, Sandra, Inca, Ani, Dairijav, Herbert, Rafa... And the others that genuinely hold me in affection! To those, you know who you are, that held me and encouraged me to keep writing in between changing nappies for Duncan and all things full time mums do, without any help. While I was also personally in the middle of a storm.

I would like to thank Trevor Greenfield, Moon Books and John Hunt Publishing for the opportunity to share this book. To Judika Illes for kindly writing the Foreword for my book, what an honour. To my wonderful friend Kia, to Sara and Victoria for reviewing the manuscript. To Josefina Morell for her wonderful front coverartwork, The Path of the Bones, and her wee illustrations. To David Rankine for providing annotations to his last book, *The Grimoire Encyclopaedia*, before it was published. Also, for pointing me in the direction to investigate scrimshaw. To Philip Shallcrass — Greywolf, Autumn Stormcaller and Rev. Aaron Davis, C. the Druid from the Chiltern Hills and Imelda Almqvist for responding to my questions in the interview and sharing so openly. To Melusine Draco for her contribution about the Hand of Glory. I'm thrilled you all are in some way part of this book too. To Constantin for his information on the magical use of shells in Greece and to everyone else that has contributed in one way or the other.

Foreword

As a writer devoted to the magical arts, what fascinates me most are those primal and often primordial topics shared by all human beings, what we might call that old bone knowledge. Bone wisdom bypasses the brain. Some knowledge is "in our bones."

Nothing unites us more than bones. After all, we all have them. We are never not in contact with bones, if only our own. They are quite literally our framework. However, the topic of bones is so much more profound than that. Let me give you a little taste of the feast of bones that Ness Bosch has prepared for you in her brilliant, comprehensive, and insightful book, *Sacred Bones, Magic Bones.*

Wherever you are, you must leave yourself open to the possibility that you are walking over bones. Human history goes back to an almost unfathomable age. As an example, the human remains found within Austria's Dragons Cave (*Drakenhöhle*), renowned for its vast number of cave bear bones, are believed to date as far back as 65,000 years. We are all of us miracles: to be alive means that *all* of your ancestors — every one of them — managed to survive long enough to reproduce and also that someone protected and cared for helpless babies and children.

People live and people die. The earth is filled with bodies, human and otherwise, some buried with care and ritual, even pomp and circumstance; some surreptitiously hidden away, and others unceremoniously dumped. Some are remembered and some long forgotten. Bones have a way of reappearing, however. There is a permanency to them. Even when everything else has been reduced to ash, sand, or dust, bones or bone fragments persist.

Bones speak. They testify and bear witness. Sometimes bones scream. In *Sacred Bones, Magic Bones*, bone woman (*huesera*) Ness Bosch writes eloquently of the mass graves of her native Spain.

This is not a history I was taught in school, and I am grateful for the lesson. But mass graves are not something foreign or "other" — there are mass graves on every continent inhabited by humans. Basically, where there are people, there will be mass graves.

We should all be aware of these graves, whether the bones are buried and rendered invisible, such as at Babi Yar (*Babyn Yar*), a ravine in Kyiv, where Nazis murdered almost 34,000 Jews in September 1941 or whether they are visible and on display as at the memorial park at Choeung Ek, built over the site of a mass grave and intended to memorialize those murdered by the Khmer Rouge in Cambodia's Killing Fields. Mass graves or unmarked graves are created, hidden, and discovered constantly. They are not things of the past. In October 2022, just shortly before I wrote this foreword, a recent mass grave was discovered in Malawi, believed to contain the remains of dozens of Ethiopians, victims of human trafficking.

Bones speak, even when people can no longer do so. Mass graves reveal secret histories of slavery and inhumanity in the Americas and Australia. In late spring 2021, for example, ground penetrating radar revealed and confirmed the existence of over 750 mass graves in western Canada containing the remains of Indigenous children, some as young as three, who had been forcibly taken from their homes and sent to residential schools, where they perished.

Not all bones reveal such heartache. Sometimes bones reveal secrets now unknown to us, if only because they happened so long ago. Ever since people have been born, they have also died. What to do with the remains has been a major metaphysical and mundane issue ever since.

The story of bones is about more than death and morbidity, however. They are equally about life and living. We typically envision prehistoric people living in caves, but the earliest documented human structures — and thus the earliest documented examples of architecture — are built from mammoth bones. Several of these bone huts have been found in Central and Eastern Europe; the earliest dates to approximately 23,000 BCE. The first time I saw a life-size replica of one of these bone huts at the American Museum of Natural History in New York City, I was a young child. I probably saw it around the same time as I heard my first Baba Yaga story, told to me by my mother. Having seen that bone hut, there was nothing unrealistic or surprising to me about the bone fence surrounding Baba's home. I've visited that replica many times since then, eventually bringing my own children. It still exists and, if you can, I recommend a visit.

While people have historically resided in homes crafted from animal bones, spirits reside in houses made of our bones. Currently, the most famous example of this is witch-goddess Baba Yaga's hut, surrounded by its fence of human bones, but there are others. Begtse, for example, a Mongolian guardian spirit, resides in a palace constructed of bleached human bones. Think of all the sayings incorporating bones: *bone wisdom, bone knowledge, down to the bone, bad to the bone*. These bone houses indicate that these spirits mean business and are not to be trifled with.

It's not just housing. The formidable and majestic goddess Kali wears a necklace of skulls. Mary Magdalene, the controversial, mysterious, and beloved saint, is frequently portrayed with a human skull. It's part of her official iconography. The sanctimonious explanation is that it's just a memento mori — an image to help you contemplate death — but other interpretations exist, too. Skulls and bones are emblematic of death and often used to symbolize danger, but they also represent life and lineage. As you will read in *Sacred Bones, Magic Bones*, you carry your ancestors in your bones. Some sacred beings *are* bones, such as skeleton saints like Mexico's Santissima Muerte or Guatemala's El Rey Pascual.

Bones are believed capable of transmitting the power of sacred beings and are thus treasured and protected, whether these are Christian, or the bone relics found among the cremated remains of Buddhist masters. The desire to possess and control the bones of saints has historically resulted in theft. In 828, Venetian merchants stole the remains of Saint Mark from his resting place in Alexandria, Egypt, for example.

Bones exemplify defiance, humor, and survival, as well as sacred power and secret histories. Consider the reveling skeletons of Mexican Day of the Dead art or the appearance of skeletons in some of the earliest cartoons, such as the "Skeleton Dance," the very first Disney *Silly Symphony*. These cartoon skeletons are a by-product of X-ray technology, developed at the end of the 19th century, and which first exposed skeletal structure, making it familiar and accessible in ways that it had never been before. Similarly, ever improving DNA technology allows us to identify otherwise unknown bodies and solve cold cases, even some very old ones.

I have been blessed and privileged to have participated in a working — a soul journey — led and guided by Ness Bosch. Over the years, I have participated in many such journeys, but this one was among the most profound and I still feel its reverberations. It was an ancestral working that answered many questions for me. One of the results of my participation is that I can hear Ness' beautiful voice in my head and thus the first time I read *Sacred Bones, Magic Bones*, I could hear the author as if she were reading her powerful words to me. Down to the bone: huesera Ness Bosch is the real deal. This is no superficial book, but one packed with information to ponder and insights worth gnawing on.

My blessings to you as you walk the Path of Bones.
— Judika Illes, author of *Encyclopedia of 5,000 Spells, Encyclopedia of Spirits,* and other books devoted to the magical arts.

Preface

Oh there are bones, bones, bones, bones
Bones inside of you
Bones, bones, bones, bones
More than just a few
So many you can count them
Amazing but it's true
There are bones, bones, bones, bones
Bones inside of you.
Count Von Count. (Sesame Street)

Bones, together with the elements of nature, are the building blocks of human spirituality.

The cult of bones and the cult of the ancestors is very old. It dates back long before recorded history, back to prehistoric times. The first rituals ever enacted were born around the dead. When we think of funeral rites our minds immediately go to the *Egyptian Book of the Dead* or the *Tibetan Book of the Dead*, however the first rites are not in any book or papyrus. It is the bones themselves that tell us the oldest part of this story. The archaeologists have to interpret them, as if burials were paintings and each element reveals a part of the secrets they hide.

For years I have been following the Path of the Bones. I did not look for this path, I began to follow it seeking to understand my own call to an animistic and shamanic path, without being fully aware of the whole picture and not knowing what I would find. This path took me much further than I expected ... I was born on the Island of Menorca, but I grew up in Granada, in Almuñecar, one of the oldest cities in Europe, the ancient Sexi, founded by the Phoenicians. I spent my childhood surrounded by an ancient necropolis, and not too far away, inland, was the largest concentration of Dolmens that exist in Europe. From an early age, I became deeply aware of ancient burial sites. I later learned about the significance of Prehistoric burials in the land of my ancestors. Some weekends my family and I would go looking for marine fossils in the mountains on the West of Granada. My house was so full of them that I even donated some to my school for their geology class. I roamed alone through gorges, near rivers and poplars looking for mushrooms in the wild. In the mountains you always come across bones or other animal remains. I found many bones and entire skeletons of mountain animals, also goats that roamed far away from humans to die. Maybe it is easier to work with bones when you see them often. Even back then, they called to me and fascinated me.

It may seem strange to those unfamiliar with the history of Spain, but I also grew up listening to the stories about human remains that were buried during the Spanish Civil War and the subsequent years of repression. These were the stories that you could only hear in the homes of those who had lost a family member like that or suffered political reprisals. Stories that were silenced and that still hurt today. These are wounds that time is not yet capable of closing. They remain in the collective memory and are transmitted precisely because they hurt. These bones with names and surnames are in anonymous places, in ditches and gorges, in mass graves. Their families still cry for their remains, either because they never found them or because they weren't allowed to exhume them. Modern governments are too afraid of the stories these bones have to tell and what would happen if they became public. The few mass graves that have been excavated, under pressure from associations that support the struggle of the relatives, have allowed some remains to be named. But not all those who disappeared were anonymous people. For example, many are still crying for Federico Garcia Lorca — asking for justice for the poet from Granada shot during the war. Although the location is known, attempts to find his remains have so far failed. Only his beloved moon knows where he is (He often featured the moon in his poems). Where are your bones, Federico? Although they have a sad story to tell, many of us would like to pay our respects to your bones.

As a shamaness I consider myself a fetish collector, especially of amulets. I also have a predilection for animal parts, especially bones and furs. On my last trip to Iceland, someone gifted me something very special, a piece of whale bone, which now, of course, is on my altar. I am also a collector of shells, which are the exoskeleton of crustaceans. Sometimes I teach people how to create oracles using bones and other elements that are found in nature. I am a Huesera, a Bone Collector, a Bone Woman.

My favourite Goddesses also happen to be bone collectors. There are several deities that we can relate to bones, however, I feel very close to Baba Yaga and The Cailleach. In both their stories we can find bones. The tales about The Cailleach tell that the bones she collects are from a cow that she slaughters every year. I have the impression that this is nothing more than an interpretive filter of the story, and that in reality the bones that The Cailleach collects are actually human. Of course, that is just a personal feeling. Also, with Baba Yaga, we do know the bones around her house were human, it's very clear in the tales. But I will share with you a story that might help you to understand this too.

Bones are not something out of the ordinary, yet there are still people who fear them. There were cultures that have turned the bones of their ancestors into relics, and those relics were then carried with them from one place to another. Other people buried their dead in their homes to keep them close to their heart and hearth. Bones are magical. Various traditions still use bones in their ritual practices. Just as a place is impregnated with the energy of its inhabitants, somehow the bones conserve the energy of the person they once belonged to. How many bones and relics are still in churches receiving thousands of visitors today? Countless tourists are mesmerised by mummies in museums worldwide. Who do you know who doesn't wish to go to Egypt to visit the Pyramids and the Valley of the Kings?

For me, and many others, bones entail power. We know that human bones are stolen for magical purposes. While I do not include human bones in my practice, many others do. I would not use bones belonging to a stranger. Nor would I want a stranger to use the bones of my ancestors. There are many types of rituals related to bones, however, it is a personal choice to work with them. We can also do it with respect for the spirit they belong to. I prefer to work with spirits as my allies, not turn them into my servants because I have their bones. But that's part of my magical ethics. I particularly like working with animal bones, because they bring the energy of the animal into my ritual. But I try to honour them and their magic through my work.

To work with the ancestors, you do not really need bones, especially if the work is for ourselves. We all carry our own ancestors in every drop of our blood. Just one call to the spirits, and knowing where to find them in the shamanic realms, is enough to open a door of communication. Over the years of guiding people, I have witnessed many stories. Although it is true that the past is the past, we can still heal the patterns, blocks and fears inherited from our ancestors. The key for our own healing is to understand the story of those who came before us. We have the tools to speak to them, even to those who lived thousands of years ago, and we can learn from their history. This information will help us to understand how a pattern that originated with them can still be conditioning us. We are the heirs of their legacy of blood and bones. Winter is the season of the bones and the ancestors. It is also the season of my beloved Baba Yaga and The Cailleach. The path to the ancestors starts in Autumn, a time to prepare and balance ourselves, a time to reconnect with the land, with nature, to the wild, a time to listen to the invisible (we tend to be too busy during summer to do this). Once we enter Winter, it is a time to connect with ourselves through our ancestors, and a time to heal and learn from the wisdom of those who preceded us. Bones leave a trail that we can follow, it is up to us to find and walk the Path of the Bones to the entrails of our own history.

Ness Bosch, January 2022.

PART I

Chapter 1

Introduction

The Path of the Bones belongs to no one and to everyone. The Path of the Bones only understands bones: the structure of what we are and what sustains us. It is a path of recognition and connection. Beneath the skin, and beyond physical, linguistic or cultural barriers, you and I are made of the same essence, and we are held together by the same skeleton. In a world full of barriers, ones we have to jump to relate to one another, bones speak a universal language that connects us. To explore that connection, we are going to have to take a look at different aspects related to bones. We are also going to explore various traditions, deities that are linked in one way or another to bones, as well as exploring some magical uses, but there is so much more to bones. Bones have many stories to tell. So many that it would be impossible to tell them all in one go. So many of these stories are still unknown to us, because they are buried. Perhaps they are waiting for someone to bring their bones to light, on the other hand, perhaps some bones were hidden so well that they will never be found. Those are the bones that scream in silence, from the blackness of secrecy or injustice.

Bones still have a lot to teach us, not only about human beings as a species, but also about the evolution of other species. Every time a new type of hominid is discovered, it causes quite a stir in the scientific community, with scholars having to relearn what they thought they once knew. That is the lesson of the bones: forget what you think you know. The interpretations of others can be wrong, unlearn your preconception of being and of yourself. Bones clearly ask you: Who are you? They put you against the wall, laugh at you, and say: "No, don't tell me what you think you are, come to me, come to your bones, let me tell you where you come from. Let me show you the masks you wear, and allow me to guide you through the veils of illusion". Bones laugh at the racist who takes a DNA test to prove his white supremacy and gets an unwanted outcome; bones also cry in some ways. Sometimes, they scream. If you have spent a night close to a cemetery, or somewhere where human remains lie, you know what I am talking about. There is an energetic imprint, a memory in the bones, as if they were files in a library. The reality is that the bones tell us many stories that belong to all of us and although they may seem alien to you, they are not. I'm going to try to share some of those bone stories hoping they somehow draw a connecting line for you. Because it is important to reconnect with our bones, it is important to connect with our identity, especially when we live in a society where individual identity tends to be lost in favour of the community. (Sometimes it is also lost because those who dare to go against the swim, against the current, are punished or marginalised at a social level.) It is an artificial society in that it creates artificial realities to house us as humans. Humans who are afraid of the forest or the wild but who plunge into a virtual jungle without giving it much thought, because we follow the murmur of the masses while we are unable to hear the call of our bones. Yes, bones also sing songs, they tell stories from long ago that are worth listening to. If you can hear this song, take the hand of this Huesera and let me open the door to the Path of the Bones for you and share a few stories...

Chapter 2

Of Bones and Ancestors

Your Bones, My Bones

Your bones, my bones, our bones, are much more than the simple structure that holds us. Our bones are an interesting tissue, for example, we have hard bones, but also soft bones. When we are born, we have more bones but over time this number decreases. Some bones fuse with each other, so when we die, we have fewer bones.

I think it is common knowledge that bones are made of calcium, but this is not their only component. Although they have used this fact to sell to us for years that drinking milk was good for our bones. The reality is that after breastfeeding, humans have no need to continue feeding on milk, (even less with milk that is made naturally for baby animals much larger than us). Our bones are a structural amalgam composed of proteins (including collagen), calcium phosphate, salts, blood (and water as a component of that blood). Basically, we can divide our bones into two: a hard part that covers the structure and a spongy or soft part that is actually responsible for the production of new cells. If you have ever found an old bone in nature, surely you know what I mean by spongy, because it is easier to see in bones that are worn out.

Our bones are important. Not only do they help us move, they also perform other vital functions for us. They help protect vital organs like our brain, heart, and lungs, but they also play an important role on other levels. Our bones produce red blood cells, white blood cells, and platelets. They also release hormones that regulate different functions as well as releasing alkaline salts that regulate our pH. But not only do they release substances into our body, they also absorb substances, such as heavy or toxic metals. Perhaps that is why you can find out if a person has been poisoned by their bones! Bones also store fatty acids in the marrow and of course, they also store minerals.

Although we think that bones are a fixed tissue, the truth is that our bones change, year after year. When bones are repaired, they are strengthened. These changes will vary from person to person depending on, their diet, and physical activity. For example, an athlete's bones will automatically strengthen due to the stress placed on the bone tissue in a given area of the body.

During pregnancy, the woman's skeletal system suffers differently in each trimester. Back, pelvic, knee, and foot pain are common. In addition to the pain, the mother's bone density drops. This should not surprise us since there is a baby drawing nutrients from the mother's blood through the placenta. Plus, hormonal changes play a very important role also in the amount of calcium that a woman produces and her metabolism during pregnancy and lactation. During the first trimester, animal studies revealed an increase in calcium absorption through the intestine. This leads to an increase in bone density, that is, the mother stores calcium, preparing for the future demand for it by the foetus. So, bone fragility or small fractures during pregnancy are more likely linked to pre-existing low bone density before pregnancy. Furthermore, osteoporosis in women later in life is more attributed to calcium loss from past lactation rather than losses in pregnancy. The mother would lose calcium when she makes milk, again increasing its absorption by her intestine and losing bone density from her reserves.

The science of our bones is fascinating. I remember in primary school we had to learn all the bones of the body in groups. On one occasion in science class we gave the teacher a terrible fright. She opened the class door to find herself a skeleton with a tracksuit, sunglasses and an open jaw. She fell backwards and ran screaming down the corridor. I guess I might not be proud of it now, but it was fun at the time. Nowadays we see more bones or skeletons, especially on Halloween, yet there are people who are still afraid or disgusted by them. To fear bones is to fear ourselves, to despise them is to despise ourselves, because they are our teachers, they show us who we are at the core of our being, such is the beauty and gift of our bones.

The Human Genesis

The genesis of humanity is perhaps one of the most interesting stories that bones tell, because it is not only our history, but also our history as a species. Bearing in mind the fragility of scientific truths, we are going to focus on what we believe to be true today about our ancestors.

Human beings belong to the primate family, and, in this family, it is precisely the bones that define us. Monkeys and humans have prehensile fingers, as well as a thumb that makes it easier for us to pick up different objects. Another significant bone detail is the position of our eyes. Being in a frontal position, this allows us to calculate distances, amongst other things. This is what we share with other primates, since we share ancestors along the evolutionary scale. It is assumed that there was no clear separation between us until the Pliocene, and that the last common ancestor between humans and monkeys would have lived about 6 or 7 million years ago.

As a species of the same family, we also share a similar reproductive capacity. We have a limited number of offspring which are completely dependent on the mother in their early years of life. Mothers will find themselves sharing the role of carers with other mothers in the same social group. This gives rise to social behaviours that will evolve until more complex social structures are created. The story of our ancestors, the upright hominids, is a story of bones and both extinction and evolution. It is also a story that tells us of significant changes in the size of our skull. The skull size increases over time to house larger brains. Through time our jaws also get refined, and we see a reduction in the number of teeth we have. These changes occur due to changes in the diet of our species over time. Because we walk upright we can also use our hands to do more, and to explore. Each bone remnant that we discover sheds more light on the evolution of our race.

While the origin of the first human is still generally placed in Africa, new bones emerge that tell more complex stories. This is until we find ourselves divided into two main groups: the Neanderthals and the Sapiens. Although others, such as the Denisovans, are also added to the equation. For years we believed that both main groups only shared space and time until the extinction of the first group. However, now we know that hybridization occurred between both species, and that we have a significant percentage of Neanderthal DNA still surviving in modern man.

When I went to school, teachers taught that reproduction between both species had not occurred. Today we know that mixed family groups were more common than previously thought when the first hybrid remains began to emerge. In fact, Neanderthals were far more than just the rough, thick-boned humans that were first introduced to me by my history teacher.

The Cave of the Bones: Atapuerca

There are several bones that teach us of our history. Sometimes it can be an individual bone or a small group of bones, while other times it is a single tooth that has a great story to tell us. There is a cave in Iberia that is of special importance to the scientific community, precisely because of the number of stories that have emerged from that cave in relation to us as a species.

Atapuerca is a mine of information. The findings in that cave have rewritten what we once knew about the population of Europe. We used to believe our first European ancestors were here over 500,000 years ago. The findings at Atapuerca taught us a different story, as it gave us the bones of older Europeans, which dated back to 780,000 years ago. Plus, more recently, a jaw has been found that dates back to 1.2 million years ago at the same site. This leads us to speculate that Europeans could be much older. In regards to what this teaches us: the bones speak. This can also be seen in the discovery of the new species of hominid — *Homo antecessor* — which was also found among the remains of other hominids in Atapuerca.

Atapuerca is a mecca for those that study the evolution of humans and of prehistoric remains. It is as if each cavity of the cave were an independent book full of stories that range from the dawn of humanity in the Iberian Peninsula and Europe, until Roman times. That's a lot of stories in just one place. Not only were there human bones found in this sacred place, but also animal bones, as well as various tools and cave paintings.

To give you an idea of the importance of this site: 85% of all the postcranial bones from the Middle Pleistocene period that have been found in the world come from Atapuerca. The site tells us the story of a cave with different sinkholes. Some of them were deadly traps for animals that later served as food for our ancestors. Other sinkholes were shelters for cave bears and other carnivores of the time.

While large parts of Europe in the Middle Pleistocene were mostly covered with ice, Iberia was not. For years it was thought that the oldest individual in Europe came from the Boxgrove site in the British Isles some 500,000 years ago. Atapuerca taught us that this was not the case, Atapuerca somehow calls out to us to look towards Iberia, which is often ignored by scholars from Northern Europe. Each discovery shows us the site's importance in the genesis, not only of the population of the continent, but also European culture throughout the different periods.

Atapuerca still hides many secrets. One of them involves 28 members of a Homo Heidelbergensis group who were deposited in the cave, all of whom died at the same time. The hypotheses for this mass grave range from the result of an epidemic, to a possible collective massacre. Scientists were also able to find evidence of a murder from 430,000 years ago, perhaps the earliest known murder. The Skull, number 17 in the archives, was fractured into 52 pieces, and reveals that the victim died from two strong impacts to the head, and was then deposited in the cave. Let's hope that with time some of these secrets will be revealed. Atapuerca will undoubtedly continue to surprise us.

The Man of Orce

40 years ago, the remains of what we know today as the oldest Europeans were discovered in the town of Orce in Granada. This discovery was surrounded by great controversy.

They were discovered by Josep Gilbert, a student at the time, in 1982. However, the climate in post-dictatorship Spain meant his discovery was subsequently discredited by colleagues and politicians. Gilbert discovered the fragment of a skull from a hominid living 1.5 million years ago in Venta Micena. That is, far older than the remains now found in Atapuerca. But as happened to the discoverer of the Altamira Cave, Marcelino Sanz de Sautuola, the discovery in Orce was discredited. It was even claimed that the bones found corresponded to the remains of a donkey and Gilbert was expelled from Orce and shamed publicly by the press and politicians. Gilbert, like Sanz, died with his work greatly disputed and without any recognition. This year marks the 40th anniversary of the discovery and we see some light finally being shed on the importance of the remains and of the Orce deposit. The skull fragment found by Gilbert was not the only ancient bone to come out of Orce. But once the past disputes hit the media, many doubted these discoveries.

However, a study of the fossil proteins in Orce's bones left no room for doubt. They were not only from a hominid, but also this hominid surpassed in antiquity any remains found in Europe to date. Plus, beyond this, it also supports the theory of the arrival of humans in Europe through the Strait of Gibraltar. Other remains with similar morphologies to the one found by Gilbert came to light, but Venta Micena in Orce still requires adequate funds for further study. The bones of the place still have many stories to tell, but Josep Gilbert will no longer be able to hear them. Unfortunately, for political and perhaps economic reasons, the Orce deposit does not have adequate financing, nor is it really given enough publicity, whilst Atapuerca continues to get most of the attention and money. In this sense, the province of Granada has always been marginalised by the central policies of Madrid. A province so rich in archaeological remains lacks the money to study or protect them, or to prevent them from being plundered by treasure hunters. This happened in several of the Phoenician Necropolises on the coast of Granada and many other sites scattered throughout the province. On a personal level I sincerely hope that this man is recognized, even if it is posthumously. His work and his legacy deserve to be commemorated. His only sin was to make a very important discovery in Spain, at a very delicate political moment. I don't think the wider world is really aware of what Spain was like during the dictatorship and in the years that followed the dictator's death. Spain is still governed by a constitution that was dictated by Franco from his deathbed, I think that says plenty. Gilbert suffered political punishment and I would like to see the name of Orce and the discoverer of the Man of Orce where they deserve to be.

Death and Ritual in Prehistoric Times

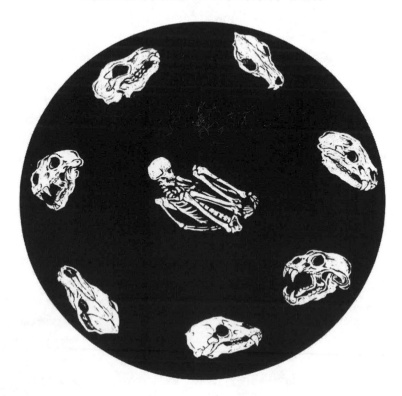

We know with certainty that the first ritual practices were born around death. We know that our ancestors, the Neanderthals, were the first to carry out burials: an act that clearly denotes a concern for the afterlife and the destiny of the human soul. In the Neanderthal burials we find the ritual component clearly identified, not only in the position of the human remains and the grave goods, but also in the remains of food, hunting tools, pollen and flowers found next to those bones. All of which point towards a ritual preparation. As part of these treasuries, we sometimes find bone remains of animals, sometimes surrounding the human remains in a circle, as if acting as a shield. Other bones found in these burials include goat horns in the East and in Europe. We also find cave bear remains, especially skulls. Archaeologists studying the Grotte de Cussac (Cave of Cussac) in Dordogne, France, found very curious human burials, not least because of the depth at which they were found. Research concluded that the remains were deliberately placed in old bear hibernation nests. Humans had left their dead there long after the bears left the cave for good. The locations where the dead were deposited indicate that the places were not chosen at random. These remains and others confirm the importance of the bear for these prehistoric people, as they entrusted their dead to the animal in one way or another.

While at first, the Neanderthals were considered less evolved hominids, their funerary practices tell us of a group with beliefs structured around death, who prepared and provisioned their loved ones for the journey beyond life. Over time, other types of humans adopted these practices making them their own. Human burials would become more elaborate, and would evolve with time. The elements of the treasuries also tell us about the status of an individual within the social group. This detail will later mark the beginning of funerary cults and with important burials, new artistic expressions and funerary monuments would rise to existence.

The Bat Cave in Albuñol and Its Treasures

In the year 1857, one of the richest prehistoric archaeological sites in the province of Granada was discovered in the town of Albuñol. It was a group of local miners who discovered the remains whilst working in the Cave of Bats. They unearthed the remains of 68 individuals and various grave goods were also found, including a solid gold diadem, made by fusing gold nuggets with a hammer. We have to be aware that this diadem was fabricated during the Neolithic period, we are not in the Age of Metals yet, which makes it even more precious. This and other discoveries in the area show clearly that locals wore bracelets and jewellery made of gold and silver, long before metals were noted in history. Unfortunately, after the discovery and notification to the authorities, the place was plundered by the miners themselves who, encouraged by the discovery of gold, tried to find more, causing great damage to the deposit. When an expert finally arrived, Manuel de Gongora y Martinez, he tried to recover what he could of what they had left behind. Manuel, although graduating in Law, had a love for archeology and was one of the few experts of the time. Because of the importance of his discoveries, he was appointed as an associate member of the Archaeological Institutes of Rome, Berlin and Paris in 1866. He found in the site in Albuñol, several esparto grass baskets. This grass is very common in the Alpujarras and the Sierras of Granada in general. He also found remains of individuals still wearing prehistoric sandals, also made of esparto grass. The craft of esparto grass has been very important throughout the millennia in Granada. My grandfather José worked with it and made slingshots and baskets, although there are few esparto artisans left in Granada today. They also found at the Cave of the Bats a very large number of poppy seeds among the offerings, which experts have interpreted as an offering part of a ritual related to eternal sleep and death. Remains of this trousseau from Albuñol can be visited in the Archaeological Museum of Granada, along with other treasures from prehistory in the province.

Neve's Grave

At the end of 2021, the news broke to the media about the discovery of what is to date, the oldest child burial ever found. Neve (as she was named by the archaeologists who found her), lived just after the last Ice Age, about 10,000 years ago. From the funerary artefacts found next to her, it has been possible to interpret that despite her young age (it is estimated that she would only be between 40 or 50 days old), she was recognized as a member of the group. Neve is the oldest female baby ever found in Eurasia, and her burial is special for numerous reasons. They left with her little body about 60 perforated shells, some pendants and an owl-eagle claw. Some of these artefacts still contained traces of ocher. A curious and important fact about Neve's burial is that some of these shells showed clear signs of great wear, so they tell us that they belonged to other members of the group and that they were given to her. It is these offerings that imply she was important to the group of hunter gatherers, even though she was such a small baby. In the town of Vedbæk in Denmark, the remains of another baby were found. This baby seemed to be a premature male child, buried approximately 6,000 years ago with his mother, who most likely died in childbirth. The peculiarity of the baby burial is that this child was deposited on the wings of a swan. Although this was not the only tomb discovered with a mother who died during childbirth and her baby, the burial with the swan's wings became the most famous of the site. Other bodies of babies buried alone were also found in the burial site, which tells us about a fairly high mortality rate during childbirth of both babies and their mothers.

Coloured Bones in Prehistory

Ocher tells us the oldest magical story. A story that still debates the theory that in the Middle Palaeolithic there could have been a cult of the Cave Bear in Europe. Ocher markings on the bear skulls and bones, and the arrangement of these at various sites, leave the door open to this possibility. When Marcelino Sanz de Sautuola discovered the Altamira Caves and raised the possibility of prehistoric origins of the paintings, he was the target of criticism and ridiculed by society at the time. Later it would be proven that his theory was true, elevating Altamira as the Sistine Chapel of Cave Art, but his discovery was buried in judgement and criticism.

In the case of the Cave Bear cult, it may also be a matter of time. The ceremonial use of red ocher in human burials has already been accepted. If a cult of the Cave Bear had arisen at that time, it would undoubtedly be linked to the principles of totemism, perhaps even to rites of passage. The coloured bones found in France, Belgium and Germany have made it clear that they were painted on purpose. The Bear would not only have been food to be hunted, but also a fierce and strong opponent. Hunting a bear would have been a challenge for boys who want to become men in the eyes of the group. We know there was a bear cult in Altai, Siberia. We also know of contemporary tribal cultures with a close relationship between humans and bears. Apart from decorating their bones, several Native American tribes speak of legends of bears transforming into men and marrying women or kidnapping them. For some people it was taboo to eat the meat of the animal, given the resemblance between humans and bears, especially once the skin is removed from the beast. In contrast, for other cultures, eating the meat of the bear would be a means of obtaining its strength. So, it would not be unreasonable to consider that Palaeolithic humans may also have wanted to honour this animal in their own way.

Ritual and Religious Evolution

Without being able to give an exact date when humans begin to perform more staged or elaborate rituals, we can state the first rituals are born close to, or at the start of, natural cycles, and are commonly designed as rites of passage. They can also be found around death, hunting, healing or fertility rites in the first agricultural societies.

The appearance of writing already brings us concise information about ritual practices and religious evolution. Though we must be mindful that it is always linked to the particular interpretation of the translator. In the Sumerian Tablets we find the first Gods, related to the waters, agriculture, natural phenomena, the stars and the great mysteries that have captivated humans from the very beginning. Those early Gods were closer to the universe and its mysteries than to man. This fact is also clearly appreciated in different native cosmologies of the American continent.

Humanity according to the first myths was a creation of the Gods. In fact, in various locations in the world, there are similarities on how the Gods create the human race. Often from the same element: mud. In the more complex societies, religious festivals of a non-funeral nature were also nationalised. The population lived by complex calendars of seasonal cults guided by the religious elite. Whilst in other societies, the responsibility of spiritually guiding the group fell on the priest- doctor of each tribe.

As for our ancestors, death and the afterlife continued to be the dominant theme for many societies. Funerary art became a state affair leading us to a popular example: absolutely everyone knows what an Egyptian pyramid is: tombs of Egyptian royalty.

Burial sites tell us about the person they house: their status, their work, and what they were known for. Tombs have been speaking to us even before the birth of writing. The treasury and clothing, the accessories or jewellery, the offerings, the tools that they left with their owner; they all have something to say. It is clear that a funerary stela already tells us much more, but let us remember that all bones speak. From those found at the bottom of a Cenote, a dolmen hidden in some corner of Europe, those found wrapped in simple linen in the desert to those in the great tomb of a Pharaoh.

Eternal Life and Mummification

It is intriguing how our ancestors, across the various latitudes of the planet, at some point coincide in their concern of preserving the body, so that it can continue to house the soul in the afterlife. When we think of mummies we automatically go to Egypt, but in reality, we find mummified bodies in many different parts of the planet; present throughout the Canary Islands, the Americas and Siberia. Each mummy tells us a story, a process.

The processes to preserve the body have evolved over millennia. In Egypt, the purpose was to preserve the Gods, since the kings and queens were considered to be Gods walking among men. The practice was later followed by the elite nobles and politicians with means. Furthermore, in the Kingdom of Kemet, not were the people mummified, but their sacred animals were preserved by this process as well.

Mummies are not something bound to our past. There are contemporary historical figures that have been preserved in this day and age, such as the remains of the Russian politician and revolutionary leader, Lenin, or Eva Peron, wife of the Argentine dictator Juan Peron. During the Middle Ages the cult of relics meant the remains of martyrs and saints proliferated all over Europe. But, the most intriguing place connected to mummification is not in Egypt, it is actually in the city of Palermo in Sicily: The Catacombs of the Capuchin Monks, that house more than a thousand mummies. That is a lot of mummies in a single place.

The Oldest Mummy

The mummy that is believed to be the oldest in the world is not found in Italy or Egypt, nor in South America. In the 1960s, mummies believed to be more than 8,000 years old were discovered in southern Portugal. If the dating is correct, they would be surpassing the oldest Egyptian mummies and even those of the Atacama Desert in Chile. According to the research, these mummies would have been dissected following a careful process and tied after death to maintain a certain posture. It is thought that the position of the mummy would have been rectified several times in order to compact the body, it is believed, to facilitate their transport. One curious fact about this find is that the photos were found in some undeveloped photo reels that were discovered by chance among the belongings of the Portuguese archaeologist Manuel Farinha dos Santos, who died in 2001. I presume that perhaps older mummies will be found in the future, but at this very moment the mummies of the Sado Valley in Portugal are the oldest ones.

Knucklebone or Astragalus

Perhaps the most popular bone of antiquity is the astragalus or talus in Latin, a bone in the lower part of the ankle, responsible for you being able to move, stand, and walk. So, it is a very important bone for us vertebrates. It is thought to be part of a game. We have also found these bones in ancient times linked to oracles, and as part of grave goods, throughout the Mediterranean, from Egypt, the Middle East, as well as Greece, Italy and Iberia. There are several tombs that have been discovered with a considerable number of astragalus.

Herodotus attributed the origin of the astragalus to the Libyans, while Plato suggested that its origin lay in Egypt, particularly as an invention of the Egyptian God Toth himself. Today it is believed that it was a practice imported from the Middle East, which spread to different latitudes, and was subsequently found in different archaeological contexts. Astragalus bones have been found in caves and sanctuaries, but also in necropolises, tombs, and houses, making clear their integration into everyday life.

It was a game that was played amongst both children and adults. You can find various representations of women and girls playing the game and it is likely men also played. There would have been several ways to play the astragalus, each side would have had a value. Something like a primitive dice. They would also have been thrown to the ground like marbles and so perhaps we find the origin of marbles in some of the forms of the game. But their value went beyond a simple game, they were highly valued objects. So much so, that they were even offered as a prize and as stated above, formed part of a funerary trousseau.

Aside from the game, astragalus were also used as oracular tools. After formulating a question to ask the gods (or a certain god) and proceeding to throw the bones — the gods would somehow speak through them. Representations of this type of oracle have been found on ancient coins. In their oracular form, astragalus have been associated with Eros and Aphrodite, the Greek and Roman Gods of love and sex.

Chapter 3

Bones and Folklore

No one can deny humanity's fascination with bones. They are one of the oldest collectable items. They are also possibly one of the earliest magical implements. The belief that bones contain the strength or energy of the animal or person they belonged to, has survived throughout history, including in Christian cults. There are many stories to be told regarding the beliefs or folklore that originated around bones and we're going to explore some of them.

Bones and Oracles

Divination is a ritual practice that has been used for thousands of years to try to predict future events or somehow decipher messages from the invisible world. Taking into account that it was usually the elite who controlled, or had access to, such occult information, the use of oracles was normalised and ensured and secured their positions of power. The first oracles are thought to have been created from bones, giving rise to what is known as osteomancy: the ability to predict the future or interpret signs using bones. The bones were cleaned and used to form an oracle set, which were then thrown in order to be interpreted. We also know of practices in which people read bones that have been burnt. The different marks or cracks in the bones had different meanings.

Without a doubt, the most famous oracle bones are those found in China, whose use dates back to the Shang Dynasty. Bones were also read in Mongolia, Japan, several countries in Africa and others in Europe. This story of bones that speak is universal.

Slinnairachd:
Blade Bone Divination in the Scottish Highlands

Using blade bones for divination is a tradition associated with the Highlands, there are mentions of similar practices in other parts of Scotland, such as the Isles of Lewis or Skye. Romantic writer, Sir Walter Scott, mentions this custom in his writing as a cultural heritage of the druids in Scotland. But other researchers have made a possible connection with divinatory practices once used by Celts and Romans. We do find blade bones oracles in ancient Greece and Rome, also in Mongolia and ancient China. This divination system is believed to have been popular also along the Silk Road. There is a similar divination system in Canada, where some of the native tribes also burned the bones before interpreting them, just like in the Highlands.

Blade Bone divination was carried out in the Highlands on certain dates, such as Christmas, New Year and other special occasions. The sacrifice of the animal would have been made in honour of the person whose fortune was to be read in the bones. After killing the animal, the meat was used, trying never to touch the bone with the knife or the teeth. After the banquet, the shoulder blades would be cleaned by boiling or burning them. After cooking the bones, it was normal for marks to appear on them; cracks, discoloration or stains. Each of those marks would symbolise something for the person interpreting the bones. Factors such as the orientation of the marks and the length would also be taken into account to determine the fate of the person.

Dragon Bones

It is common knowledge that China is linked to dragons. It is not only a symbol of imperial power but also a link we find in different myths. Dragons are not only a symbol of identity for the Chinese people, they are also medicine. Dragon bones are used as a remedy in traditional Chinese medicine. It is not known exactly when this remedy began, however, we do know that they are not really dragon bones, but fossils of dinosaurs and large mammals. The first mention of the use of dragon bones is found in Chinese medicinal treatises from the first century CE.

In later treaties, bone properties began to be differentiated depending on their colour. They were put into one of five groups which is typical of traditional Chinese medicine. Elemental natures and types of healing mushrooms are also grouped into five. The use of dragon bones spread to other territories making these bones more and more precious.

The fossil origin of these dragon bones was not studied until the end of the 1800s by Europeans. Fascinated by traditional Chinese medicine and its remedies, they were curious and tried to decipher the origin of the famous dragon bones. Following the trail of these bones, they not only discovered different fossil mines in various towns, but this search led to the discovery of the famous "Peking Man", proving the presence of a new hominid genus in Asia.

The Bones of My Enemies

Not all the stories connected to the bones can be filtered out and spoken openly about. In prehistoric times, we find burials that reveal violent deaths. The fight for territory, hunting, and overall history of humanity also has black holes and dark stories. Not all of them were written in the modern age or during modern conflicts. The reality is that the bones of our enemies are powerful. They are powerful in that they are vessels of that enemy's vital energy. The history of head-hunters is not unique to the tribes that shocked Victorian society at the turn of the century. There is much power to be obtained in the acquisition of your enemy's bones. These bones can be used to curse an entire family lineage. As a curiosity, there is a tribe in Papua, the Chimbu, who paint their bodies as if they were skeletons to scare their enemies.

Scrimshaw

Scrimshaw is the bone and ivory art produced by whaling sailors around the world. We find the roots of scrimshaw in the practices of indigenous peoples who decorated bones and ivory from animals. Possibly the white man had already come into contact with this type of tribal art throughout the centuries of conquest and exploration of territories. Some scholars find in the art of the natives from the Islands of the Pacific or the Inuit people, the link to the origin of scrimshaw as an adaptation of the native techniques by western sailors.

Scrimshaw, within the universal art of bone carving and decoration, specifically refers to the art created by whale hunting sailors during the 19th Century and into the 20th Century. Sailors were condemned to spend long periods at sea. With few leisure options, it is believed that they began this practice to kill time on board. It was a practice condemned by their superiors who accused them of being time wasters or lazy, instead of working. In fact, it is believed that the term scrimshaw would literally mean wasting time. Although the teeth of the sperm whale were the most popular material to make Scrimshaw out of, other bones and parts of the whale were also used, along with other materials from the sea such as walruses' teeth, turtle shells and seashells.

Commercial whaling was banned in 1986, although not all countries accepted the new laws. Japan, Norway and Denmark have continued to hunt for commercial purposes, under pressure and judgement from other countries and environmental associations. We must remember whaling is not a modern practice. We find mentions as far back as the classical era about cetacean hunting; it had its peak from the 16th century, reaching the 20th century. The industry flourished with the industrial revolution and the construction of modern whaling ships. These technologies meant an increased number of whaling ships and the abusive hunting of animals, putting various species in danger of extinction. This led to the first prohibitions from 1969 onwards, concluding with the definitive prohibition in the year 1986.

Subsequently the ban on commercial whaling has affected the practice of scrimshaw. From the prohibition, an important need has arisen to preserve the history of the whaling culture and scrimshaw is part of that. Thus, it is a key feature in museums dedicated to remembering this industry.

Today scrimshaw is still relatively unknown although it is currently seeing a resurgence, especially among artisans who work with bone. Not only do we find different websites dedicated to scrimshaw, but it is also found in shops. Many people are interested in learning this traditional art.

Shells and Conch Shells

Shells have been used by humans since ancient times. Shells were used in tools and were one of the first currencies. Various peoples around the world would have used them as proto-money. Shells were used to adorn clothes and we find reminiscences of these prehistoric practices in some indigenous groups and peoples who, even today, continue to use shells in their ceremonial costumes or regalia. Shells were used to create accessories and musical instruments.

As exoskeletons, the use of shells and conchs is clearly linked to their physical qualities. In Greece, shells are used for their protective properties in various ways. The shells are crushed and the resulting powder is used, sometimes mixed with sea salt, to create circles of protection. This shell dust can also be mixed with brick dust, in this case to create protective circles for the house.

The use of shells to create protective musical instruments has been used since prehistoric times. In Greece, shell wind chimes still have that protective character. They were hung outside the house, near the windows or doors so that when moved by the sea breeze, the sound would drive away evil spirits and attract protective spirits.

We find a similar use of shells in other places such as Malta, Sicily and the Balearic Islands, where shells were used as instruments to make sound signals. These marine trumpets had different names throughout the Mediterranean and Portugal, such as Birambao, Berimbau, Bronja, Brogna or Bourou. They are similarly used in Hawaii and Tahiti. In this sense, the use of shells is universal and widespread — been used by people who lived both by the sea and inland.

In the North of Spain, there are houses covered with shells in Galicia and Asturias. I remember being amazed at those houses on our family trips to Galicia. There is also a small chapel on the island of La Toja, completely covered with scallop shells. In ancient times they were used as containers, in a ritual context, as marine bowls to make offerings and to burn incense. The use of a shell by the Pilgrims who walk the Camino de Santiago, is linked in some way to the protective qualities of the shells. Today the scallop shell is the symbol of the Camino — it is the emblem of the pilgrims and is used to mark the route along the way.

Also linked to the pilgrims of Santiago de Compostela, there was a custom in Kent in the south of England, although there are also testimonies of this custom in Essex, Sussex, Hampshire and Swansea, of building small grottos with shells on the beach, illuminated with candles. Although initially this tradition had begun as an offering made by people who could not visit Santiago on pilgrimage, it seems that by the 18th century, the religious connotations had disappeared. What followed was a tradition carried on by children, who then asked for donations or alms for their Grotto. Sadly, this convention almost died out in the mid-20th century but places such as Whitstable and Margate are successfully trying to revive the tradition.

Teeth Folklore

Teeth have been fetishes that have accompanied us since ancient times. Proof of this is noted in a Mesolithic tomb in Sweden, where a rattle made with wild boar teeth was found next to the remains of a mother and her baby. Also Russian Stone Age graves containing rattles were discovered and closer to us in time, we find tooth rattles in tribal societies in British Columbia, Hawaii and Alaska.

Deer, Elk and Wild Boar teeth have been found sewn to clothes. Sometimes these are combined with shells, like beads. According to the position of the archaeological remains found, they would have decorated pectorals, arms, legs and even belts. At the Skateholm site in Sweden, archaeologists found a baby sling or carrier decorated with teeth. But the use of the teeth would not have been merely decorative, it would have had a spiritual, protective meaning.

We can reach this conclusion by analysing a custom from the island of Timor, where the inhabitants of the highest castes decorate the baby slings with Tiger or Leopard teeth, to protect the baby from evil. The sound would not only be calming the baby, it would also ward off evil spirits.

Moving into the context of the folklore surrounding human teeth, we are going to explore Milk Teeth. The first thing of interest is that the name of 'milk teeth' is global; that is to say that we find the same meaning in languages such as French, English, Spanish, Russian and German. Such names refer to the mother's milk or the mother's breast, as in the Altai, where milk teeth are known as Woman's Breast Tooth.

The customs in relation to the teeth are also widespread. In the South of Spain and other countries, mothers save their children's milk teeth as they fall out. I have done it, as my mother did. In other countries, however, the milk tooth is thrown, over the roofs, into a source of water — an act that is sometimes accompanied by a prayer — the tooth is asked to bring a new, stronger tooth. In other places they are buried, offered to the fire or thrown behind the stove. The Aino of Japan plus some people of Mongolia, Central Asia and Alaska, gave their teeth to a dog.

The teeth are also offered, in exchange for favours or money. I'm sure you have heard of the Tooth Fairy or the Perez Mouse. In other places, such as Bulgaria, Greece or regions of Ancient Anatolia, it was a Raven that took the tooth. If we speak on a magical or spiritual level, one of the greatest offerings that can be made to a spirit would be a bone or your blood. That is why firstborns were sacrificed to some Gods.

A couple of years ago I was in Egypt during a teaching retreat I had to go and visit the dentist because of a horrible toothache. Since I didn't have much time, the dentist recommended extraction. So, he did and I kept my tooth until after the retreat. When I was able to do so, I went along the Nile River and gave it to Hapi, the God-Spirit of the river. That was my offering for him and to my ancestors from the area. When children offer their milk teeth to the Tooth Fairy or the Perez Mouse, these are supernatural beings. Those teeth are something very precious, that's why some mothers used to keep them, long before celebrities or influencers made it fashionable.

Broken Bones

Long before medical services and hospitals were regularised, before emergency rooms existed or we could make an appointment with a traumatologist, people had broken bones and someone fixed them. Although these traditions are disappearing, thanks mainly to the ease of access to public health in many countries, the folk healers or people with a "gift" to heal were, for hundreds of years, the people's doctors. The bonesetters. They were people who knew about bones and how to place them so that they would heal properly. There have been bonesetters all over the world, in different latitudes and traditions but exercising the same job, fixing bones.

Mostly self-taught, some mended both animal and human bones. Perhaps they even learned by healing their own animals, out of necessity. The art of healing bones is often passed down from father/mother to son/daughter. They learned the trade by observing and helping their parents. This hereditary knowledge was happening in many places and passed down from generation to generation. I lived in a town in the mountains, Lanjarón, in Granada, that had a bonesetter. People came to see him from different places, despite the fact that there were already hospitals. There were several healers in the area. Unfortunately, many took their knowledge to the grave, as maybe there was no one in their family interested in learning the art of bone healing. Nowadays, we can find folk healers in some remote areas, though there are not many left in Europe now. So, this figure and their knowledge has disappeared in many communities.

Lucky Bones

You may have seen a rabbit's foot hanging from a key chain for good luck, or noticed this object in a movie. The Greeks believed, and still believe, that wearing a bat bone brings good luck. But, in contrast, killing a bat for its bones was thought to bring bad luck. In old Europe it was believed that wearing a black cat bone protected against witchcraft — this superstition was associated with the belief that witches could transform into black cats. There was also a belief that a black cat bone could make you invisible, the poor black cats were cooked alive.

The clavicles of various birds are also considered lucky and it is supposed that the tradition of breaking this bone comes from the Romans or Etruscans. In the New World, the chicken or turkey clavicle is considered the quintessential lucky bone. In the Ozark Mountains it is even used to attract a mate. There is a popular belief in hoodoo, although it is believed that the origin is Native American and that it was later adopted by slaves, for which carrying the penis bone of a raccoon ensures good luck and is used as a love fetish.

Rattlesnakes in the New World

Within the folklore of the First Peoples of North America, we find that the Rattlesnake rattles were used both to calm babies and to protect oneself from snakes. Carrying a rattle prevented you from meeting snakes on your path and even prevented you from being bitten. If you rubbed a rattle in your eyes, it somehow gave you the power to see the snake before it saw you.

The Rattlesnake rattle was also considered a good luck charm for musicians. Many musicians put it inside their violins or guitars, or hung it from their banjos. Somehow it was believed that the rattle made them play better and that it would help them to attract abundance and money.

The Whitby Hand of Glory by Melusine Draco

One of the grisliest magical 'tools', found in magical spell-books or grimoires and using body parts for maximum effect, is the Hand of Glory — a dried, skeletal and pickled hand of a hanged man. Often specified as being the left (Latin: sinister) hand, or, if the person was hanged for murder, the hand that 'did the deed'. Old European beliefs attribute great powers to a Hand of Glory combined with a candle. The grimoire *Petit Albert* lists this spell, which purportedly had the power to unlock any door it came across:

Take the right or left hand of a felon who is hanging from a gibbet beside a highway; wrap it in part of a funeral pall and squeeze it well. Then put it into an earthenware vessel with zimat, nitre, salt and long peppers, the whole well powdered. Leave it in this vessel for a fortnight, then take it out and expose it to full sunlight during the dog-days until it becomes quite dry. If the sun is not strong enough, put it in an oven with fern and vervain. Next make a kind of candle from the fat of a gibbeted felon, virgin wax, sesame, and ponie, and use the Hand of Glory as a candlestick to hold this candle when lighted, and then those in every place into which you go with this baneful instrument shall remain motionless made from fat from the corpse of the same malefactor who died on the gallows.

The Whitby Hand has been at the museum since 1935, shortly after it was discovered by a local stonemason, Joseph Ford, hidden in the roof of a thatched cottage in the nearby village of Castleton. It was Ford himself who identified the hand as a hand of glory, based on his own knowledge of local folklore.

Etymologist Walter Skeat reports that, while folklore has long attributed mystical powers to a dead man's hand, the specific phrase 'hand of glory' is, in fact, a folk etymology deriving from the French main de gloire, a corruption of mandragore, which is to say mandrake — the most famous magical plant in Europe. The first mention of a 'hand of glory' in English (1707) refers to a piece of mandrake root, kept as a charm to make coins multiply, which corresponds to mediaeval French maindegloire, a corruption of Latin mandragora — 'mandrake'. The French word, however, sounds exactly as if it meant 'hand of glory' so it is commonly applied to a magical torch made from a dead man's hand to cast people into deep sleep.

Today the Hand of Glory is one of those spells that everyone respects, whatever the centuries, no matter the tradition, that feeling of respect is honoured amongst practitioners of witchcraft.

A Note on Religious Relics

We know of the existence of hundreds of relics of saints or martyrs, but the Christian religion is not the only one that worships human remains as relics. To this day thousands of pilgrims continue to visit chapels and churches to pay their respects to these remains. We can still visit some of these relics, although in reality, we cannot tell if they do in fact belong to those saints. I found out during my research that there are sites that claim to have the foreskin of Jesus Christ in their possession and that miracles were attributed to it. I prefer to reserve comment on this matter. Apparently, there are also several Buddha teeth in different places and Muslims also have relics of their prophet Muhammad. In Tibet, human bones were used to create ritual instruments. Very likely to have shamanic origin, these instruments were later adopted by Buddhist rites.

Walking Bones

Today there are still bones that walk our streets in different parts of the world. This fact shows the weight of our relationship with bones in our collective consciousness. An example of this are the different masquerades and parades where people dress up with animal bones. Mari Lwyd is a popular folk tradition from South Wales, where a decorated horse skull is paraded, held by a stick and covered with a white sheet, which also covers the person who manipulates a mechanism that makes the bones collide. But it is not the only place in the British Isles where masquerades were held — there is evidence of similar traditions in places such as Derbyshire, the Hodening in Kent and Láir Bhán in Ireland. Heads of horses, rams and goats were used, such as Handsworth's Old Tup. These traditions of the British Isles are imported from the continent, like many other cults. There are many places in old Europe where the heads of bulls, horses or goats are still paraded and these masquerades have a clear origin in the Neolithic cults of fertility, death and rebirth.

These traditional masquerades have more in common than we might expect, given the geographical distance that separates them. But we have to remember that our ancestors were great travellers and that they travelled large distances taking with them their traditions and their Gods.

Bones are used to create musical instruments to be played in the parades. In some places they use cowbells and sometimes they simply hang bones from their clothes to make noise when they collide with each other during the parade. The noise or sound being an important part of the ritual, since in some ways it was a call for both the spirits, and the rain. A clear attempt to bring heaven to earth during the celebration. The bones continue to sing this ancestral song in different regions such as Romania, Iberia, Austria, Sardinia and Bulgaria.

These celebrations coincide in some places with the ancient Roman Saturnalia, other times with the spring or early May celebrations. These folk traditions inherited from Neolithic rites, have survived in the hearts of people through the ages. They are very much alive in places like Sardinia and Iberia where the carnivals also have a connection to the Dionysian Cult. The deity travelled through the Mediterranean, thanks to the commercial contacts between Iberia and Sardinia with Crete and other colonies. But actually, these Dionysian rituals would have come to Crete from ancient Thrace (present-day Bulgaria), in the Balkans. The celebrations used to include ecstatic dances and masks, while drinking profusely to the sound of music. The God himself takes the form of bulls and goats, and we find a wide representation of these two animals in the different masquerades celebrated in the Mediterranean.

Bone Hunters Today

Although it sounds strange, tourism related to bones attracts a lot of people. Across Europe and in other parts of the world we find chapels and places full of bones that receive thousands of visits a year. There are also very famous cemeteries that are filled with tourists and are a 'must visit' in some places. For the architecture and beauty, for the people buried there, for the history — there are many reasons cemeteries attract visitors. But human bones are not the only popular ones, dinosaur and fossil remains scattered around the planet attract many people. Areas with easy access in particular are a draw for anyone who wants to spend their day fossil hunting. I am going to share with you some of those places that are popular for their bones in case you are curious.

Perhaps one of the most famous ossuaries is the Sedlec Ossuary in the Czech Republic. This place houses between 40,000 or 70,000 human skeletons. Also, in the Czech Republic we find the Zelnik Chapel that houses about 20,000 bones. Not far from there, in Kudowa-Zdrój in Poland, we find the famous Czaszek Chapel, the Church of Skulls, covered up to the ceiling with more than 20,000 bones. Though perhaps one of the most curious ossuaries in central Europe is the one in the city of Hallstatt in Austria and although it does not house a large number of bones, it is perhaps the most picturesque, since the skulls are hand-painted with symbols and floral motifs. On the other side of the border, in Germany, in the town of Oppenheim, we find in the Michaelskapelle of the Church of St Catherine, an ossuary with about 20,000 bones. To the south, in France, although we find several ossuaries, perhaps the most famous place for bones in the country is the Catacombs of Paris — a major tourist attraction in the city of light. Continuing south in Spain, we find the Wamba ossuary, very close to Valladolid. Not far from there, in the city of Evora, we find the most important ossuaries in Portugal. Continuing to the South of Europe, in Italy, we find several ossuaries in different chapels, but perhaps the most curious is the Novara ossuary in the north of the country. Not only because the chapel has the curious shape of an Egyptian pyramid, but also because of the bones it houses. They belong to the victims who perished in the battle of Novara against the Austrians. Across the Atlantic Sea, in the Americas, we find perhaps the largest ossuary at the San Francisco Convent in Lima, Peru, containing the bones of at least 70,000 people.

If you are interested in cemeteries below are my top 10 recommendations:

1. Paris. Because there are several beautiful cemeteries that you can visit, not only for their style, but also for the people buried in them. Pere Lachaise, the Cemeteries of Montparnasse and Montmartre and Sant Vicent, to name a few.
2. London and its magnificent 7. A group of private cemeteries that were built in the Victorian era on the outskirts of London: Kensal Green, West Norwood Cemetery, Highgate Cemetery (which is usually one of the most visited), Abney Park Cemetery, Brompton Cemetery, Nunhead Cemetery and Towers Hamlet Cemetery.
3. Japan. There are actually several cemeteries and shrines in the country that are worth visiting. The Yanaka cemetery is very beautiful although I am divided between Yanaka and the Fuji Cemetery which is also very special. Okunoin Cemetery is the largest cemetery

in the country and was founded in the 9th century. You've probably seen Ise Shrine in photographs or the Fushimi Inari Shrine in Kyoto. One less known shrine but striking because of its beauty is the Udo Shrine, in the Nichinan region.

4. Valley of the Kings in Egypt and the Nile Valley in general, where we can visit several pyramids and also the Necropolis in Thebes. I loved the time I spent in Egypt; there is so much to see.

5. Scotland. I have visited several really beautiful cemeteries here. The Glasgow Necropolis is very popular and don't miss the Southern Necropolis to the south of the city. Also, Greyfriars Cemetery, Old Calton, Canongate and Warriston Cemetery in Edinburgh. Others worth a mention include the Greenock Cemetery and the Irvine Old Parish Church Graveyard. As a curiosity, in Aberdeenshire, there is a pyramid erected by Queen Victoria to commemorate Prince Albert. It is located on the Balmoral Estate, owned by the Royal Family, but you can walk around the area. It is truly striking, especially because of the beauty of the landscape that surrounds it.

6. New Orleans and the St Louise and Lafayette Cemeteries. These places are a must if you are interested in hoodoo and traditions from the African Diaspora in the Gulf of Mexico.

7. Bonaventure Cemetery in Savannah, Georgia. The place has a haunting beauty, and while it is a cemetery, a home for the dead, the place is very much alive, with the vibrant flora of the area, Azaleas, Camellias, Dogwood and majestic Oak trees.

8. Rauda, the Royal Cemetery situated in the Alhambra Palace in Granada. If you wish to travel back in time, this is the place. Although after Christians took over the city, the remains of the Nasrid Royal Family were moved to

Mondujar, in the Lecrin Valley, outside Granada, so really both places are significant.

9. A Phoenician Necropolis, located on the Island of Mallorca. The Son Real Necropolis is simply spectacular.

10. Gorafe Megalithic Park. A place in Granada that houses the largest number of Dolmens in all of Europe: 240 dolmens distributed in 10 Necropolises. All this in one place. It is an absolutely fascinating place, especially if you are into archeology.

Fossils

If, like me, you like fossils, there are some places scattered around the planet that are a true paradise for us fossil lovers. Some of these places are fairly accessible and you won't need to go with a pick and shovel, you will only have to take a walk and look around to find these treasures from the past.

British Isles top 10 fossil locations

1. Dorset's Jurassic Coast is perhaps my number one place because it has an annual festival of fossils in Lyme Regis — it is a very interesting experience for the whole family.

2. The Isle of Wight is on my list because the whole island is truly a paradise for looking for fossils. It is the place with the most dinosaur remains in Europe!

3. Herne Bay in Kent County, which is famous for its abundance of fossil shark teeth.

4. Llantwit Major in Wales is great for a family day out hunting for fossils from the Jurassic period: Gastropods, Coral and Sea Urchins.

5. Dunraven Bay in Wales with its spectacular limestone cliffs.

6. Danes Dyke in Yorkshire, famous for its sponge fossils from the Cretaceous period.

7. Wemyss in Fife, Scotland. A place full of fossils from the Carboniferous period and some very interesting caves. If we follow the coast from St Andrews to Crail, we will find fossils from the same geological period and other caves to visit. The area is gorgeous.

8. Ayrshire, in Scotland. Approximately between Dunure and Girvan, towards Ballantrae we can find fossils at various points along the coast. The soil in Ayrshire is very rich, we also find fossils inland, for example, at Lady Burn, Dalmellington, Auchinleck and in the river Ayr, near Sorn.

9. Isle of Skye in Scotland, where we find Jurassic deposits and although not all have easy access, the Isle of Skye is famous for its dinosaur fossils.

10. Eastbourne in Sussex. Many call the place the paradise of ammonites, although we can also find crinoids and bivalves among the chalk walls. The cliffs have several access points and it is not too difficult to get to the beach.

In Europe

On my list of places to visit in Europe, I would start with Denmark, where we find several fossil deposits, and amber. Let's not forget that amber is actually fossilised resin! The chalk cliffs of Mons Klint, on Mon Island in the South of the country, Mariager Fjord is ideal for finding marine fossils such as urchins. If you wish to go amber hunting try on the West coast in Jutland, where you can find amber nuggets simply by walking on the beach, especially after a sea storm. Of course, I would also visit Spain. The truth is that the country is incredibly rich in fossils. The variety is enormous, as we find deposits covering different geological periods. We are going to find a bit of everything: Dinosaurs, petrified plants, marine fossils ... Geotourism is booming in the Iberian Peninsula and there are more and more companies specialising in the sector.

To highlight some of the places, the Route of the Dinosaurs in Soria, the Route of the Dinosaurs in La Rioja, the Mesozoic Dinosaur sites of La Demanda in Burgos, and Atapuerca also in Burgos. The Coast of Dinosaurs in Asturias, Dinopolis in Teruel, Fonelas Paleontological Station in Granada, which has one of the most important fossil deposits in Europe. Also in Granada, in Orce, we find the "Josep Gilbert" First Settlers of Europe Interpretation Centre. The Paleontological Museum of Elche is one of the most important in the country. Other places across Europe with fossils are: The Museum of Natural History in Berlin and the Solnhofen deposit, also in Germany, the Museum and Park of Dinosaurs in Meze, in France, also the Museum of Natural History in Paris is a great place to see dinosaurs and fossils.

Other places around the world

In North America we find several destinations famous for their fossils, perhaps the most popular fossils are in the Potomac River, where dinosaur eggs have been found. In the state of Florida is the Bone Valley, where the largest fossil remains from the Ice Age have been found. The Guadalupe Mountains National Park, in Texas, hides one of the best-preserved ancient reefs on the planet. In Utah we find the Dinosaur National Monument and the popular Fossil Discovery Trail that hides dinosaur bones and other fossils among the rock. The South of the American continent is a paradise for dinosaurs, we find them in the South in the Patagonia of Chile. Not far, in Argentina they found the largest carnivorous dinosaur — the Giganotosaurus Carolinii. We also find dinosaurs in Brazil, and in Peru we find several dinosaur deposits and footprints. Another place to visit for its fossils is Australia, which is famous for its mining deposits of opal and other minerals, but it also has very important archaeological sites, such as a Miocene deposit called McGraths Flat found in the Central Tablelands. In the 1980s the oldest fossil evidence for cellular life, dating back 3.43 billion years. was discovered on a beach in western Australia. This discovery divided the scientific community, which finally, only recently has accepted the finding of the Pilbara region as good after it was verified that the remains contain organic matter.

Chapter 4

The Bones of the Gods

The threads that bind the Gods to death and bones are ancient. Our bones, symbols of our mortality, have also been offered to the Divine.

Although this topic is still somewhat taboo among many neopagans, we know that human sacrifices were made to the Gods in the past. One of my fiercest criticisms of the community is precisely the attempt to soften and only work with the most benevolent aspects of ancient deities. Many have received sacrifices, both human and animal but many still won't accept that side of "their" Gods. Neopagans aren't the only ones who have trouble dealing with this bloody past. Some modern scholars try to deny this fact, despite the evidence of human remains found in places of worship.

Julius Caesar spoke in his chronicles of the human sacrifices among the druids and how they were fighting to end these barbaric Celtic customs. Romans also talk about the human sacrifices made by the Phoenicians and Etruscans — but they were not the only ones to perform these practices. There is archaeological evidence that points to ritual human sacrifices at different times in history and by different cultures. These range from the Mesolithic in areas of northern Europe to Mesopotamia, the Aztecs, the Shang Dynasty in China, the Norse and the Yoruba, associated with the Orisha Religion. The latter of which continued until the end of the 19th century.

Whether we like it or not, human and animal sacrifices are part of the history and worship of many of our Gods. Within our civilised minds, we may now look at the past as barbaric. However, it doesn't help anyone to paint over the traces of our bloody past with unicorns and rainbows. We cannot "veganise" the past. Yes, there were classic authors who were totally against sacrifices, but these are part of our history. We have to remember at this point that the Brahmanical religions also speak of sacrifices, also human sacrifices in their scriptures. But it seems that no one is too shocked by it! Even Jesus was sacrificed for humanity. Today these great religions continue to sacrifice animals every year for their celebrations on special dates along the year. Sacrifice is still part of their traditions but it seems more scandalous if the person who sacrifices an animal is someone who follows a religion more closely linked to the indigenous practices or if a pagan does it.

About the Nature of the Sacrifices

What is a Sacrifice? Sacrifice is a word that comes from the Latin, Sacrificium, which literally means to make sacred. A Sacrifice is an offering or gift that is given to a supernatural entity or force, either to thank, appease, honour or make some kind of exchange or payment through this act between the human and the divinity. An important point to keep in mind about the nature of the sacrifices is that they were understood within a religious or political context. These aspects are often intertwined in antiquity.Often, we can dismiss ancient chronicles or literary texts because of our modern prejudices about human sacrifice in ancient times. But not only do we find references to human sacrifices in classical texts, the Bible itself also has references to sacrifices. This should not surprise us knowing that part of the texts of the Bible are inspired by mythology and the literature of ancient Sumer, especially those belonging to the Book of Genesis. Several of its protagonists make a clear allusion to characters from the Sumerian civilization. As the Sumerians practised human sacrifice, or so it is believed, the parallels are obvious.

We find clear references to sacrifices in mythological stories, such as the one that tells us about the Minotaur of the Island of Crete. The city of Athens had to provide 14 young people (seven boys and seven girls) to be delivered to the Minotaur in Crete as a sacrifice for the monster.

We know that Crete also became a Phoenician colony and we know, from the archaeological remains found in the Phoenician city of Carthage, that they practised human sacrifice. The story of the Minotaur may just be a legend legacy from the Minoan times but we could take it as a testimony that the idea that human sacrifices were accepted and, as I said, they were a matter of state. I have already mentioned the Bible and the clues it gives about human sacrifices, but the reality is that both the Phoenicians and Israelites shared ties with the Canaanite people and ancient Sumer and the cult of Melqart/Moloch, a deity to whom human sacrifices are attributed (children and young people, to be more specific). So, the mention in the story of Theseus and the Minotaur to the sacrifices of the 14 young people could, as mentioned above, have a real basis.

We find another reference to sacrifices to the gods in mythology, in the story of Prometheus as the originator of animal sacrifices to the gods (at least in Greek mythology).

Prometheus sacrifices a large bull and from the remains he makes two different parts. Trying to benefit the humans, whom he had already been helping to survive — giving them fire — he prepares a pile with the best cuts of meat. He covers them with waste to make them look unappetizing and makes another pile with the bones of the animal, which is covered in fat and some succulent cuts of meat. Zeus, who had to choose, is carried away by deception and chooses the pile that hides the bones of the animal. Zeus, angry at this favouritism, snatches the fire that Prometheus had given to men. Once again, Prometheus, in favour of humans, who in other myths appear to be his own creation, steals the fire of the Gods. This new betrayal costs Prometheus a severe punishment. Zeus also commissions Hephaestus to create Pandora, as a carrier of diseases, plagues and old age among other things. She would be the punishment for humans. Prometheus would spend millennia chained to a mountain with his liver being devoured every day by an eagle, until Hercules killed the eagle and ended his punishment.

Of course, before Prometheus performed the first sacrifice according to mythology, we find references in Sumerian cuneiform tablets about animal sacrifices. Also, their neighbours the Canaanites would make use of ritual sacrifice in their religious practices.

Deities and Sacrifices

Far from what some people might think, these sacrifices would be made quickly and without suffering. We have to understand that something that is going to be offered to the gods cannot be loaded with pain at an energetic level, so the priests or the slaughterer would use great skill when using the knife to avoid the suffering of the animal.

Once the animal is dead, and after being bled, the skin would be delivered to the offeror. The meat and fat would be given to the gods, although priests and assistants would also participate in the offering and others would eat and be part of the feast. On other occasions the animal would be burned whole, directly on the altar, as a way of sending the animal to the gods through the smoke. The entrails of the animal would be washed and sometimes used for divination.

It is not the suffering of the animal that is offered to the Gods, to think that is a mistake. The gods don't want the pain, the gods were offered a feast. The animals would be sacrificed or burned on the altar as a celestial banquet table for the gods. We have already noted how sacrifices could be made to placate the gods, but also to get their favours or help, in an attempt to get their attention. Perhaps to obtain divine forgiveness or establish a relationship with the deity through such sacrifices. The sacrifice was an exchange between the offeror and the deity, a bridge between the profane and the sacred. Taking this into account, we do not have to see the sacrifices that were made in the past as something barbaric, but as what they were, their way of connecting with the sacred.

Altars used to be built in places where the given deity would have manifested. Other people would begin to visit the place, hoping to obtain some sign or divine communication, thus beginning the pilgrimages of worship. Over time, other public and private buildings would be built around these altars. Places of worship would become nerve centres of development. In fact, this could be the history of some ancient cities.

Deities and Bones

Although we could talk about many deities related to bones through animal sacrifices, in this section we are going to explore some deities that are directly related to bones in their stories or representations.

All of them are united by the bones, as we are, even if they come from very different traditions. Some are quite well known and others may not be familiar to you. I invite you to further explore those that in some way call to you or simply make you more curious. Just remember that before working with any deity it is important to do research.

Understanding the context of the cult is equally important. By studying the deity, we are honouring it, by showing earnestness and encouragement to approach correctly. It is important for you to understand that just because you wish to work with a deity does not mean that the deity will be interested in working with you. We do not have a direct line with whoever we want, in this sense. When it comes to divinities from traditions foreign to us or far away, think that you have to establish a bond based on your personal work and respect.

Chamunda

Chamunda is a Hindu goddess whose origin is believed to be in the Vindhya mountains in the centre of India. Her cult would have spread among the different tribes of the area. She is a warrior, a tribal goddess who is revered by some people as a deity that provides protection to the home and family. She would be a fierce and powerful aspect of the Divine Mother.

Her birth or origin occurs as an emanation from Goddess Durga during a battle with two Demons — Chanda and Munda. Chamunda emanates from Durga and defeats the Demons, so

Durga gives her name. Thus, giving it a personality independent of its own, although she also associates Chamunda with the Goddesses, Kali and Parvati. We sometimes find Chamunda depicted as a skeleton, wearing a necklace of skulls and holding a bowl of blood. Among the offerings that were made to her was liquor and sacrifices — human and also animal sacrifices. She is a Goddess associated with Death, Changes, and Time, as well as war and battle.

Cailleach

As an Iberian priestess, I find it difficult to keep it brief when writing about The Cailleach Goddess, as she is one of the Iberian Goddesses who would not only conquer the British Isles, but also become the great architect of the northern lands. Contrary to what some pagans still believe, The Cailleach is not a Deity originating from the Isles. In the writings of Herodotus (5th Century BCE), references to the Goddess Cailleach are found, as a Goddess of the Tribe of the Callaeci in Iberia.

The Cailleach is a very old Goddess, so old that in reality we find ourselves before the personification of the winter season in the area. In addition, she would represent all the meteorological phenomena of the season. And The Cailleach is also a creator Goddess of the landscape, which she models at her whim. This is how she created Scotland, but before arriving there, she also passes through Ireland where she entertains herself by modifying the landscape and creating different places. This is why the Goddess has become an important Deity in both Ireland and Scotland. Interestingly, there is a similarity between her name Beara and Beira, the name of several counties in what is now the territory of Portugal. This is highlighted in the Sierra de la Estrella, a place that speaks of her, especially in winter. It is important to record the close relationship between The Cailleach and the Witch of the East, Baba Yaga. We cannot rule out the theory that The Cailleach could be an emanation of the latter, knowing how Baba Yaga crossed Europe to the West and became such an important figure in European folklore under different names.

We find The Cailleach's relationship with bones in one of her stories. It happens that a friar asks The Cailleach her age, because he sees that she is very old. She tells him that ever since she turned 18, she has been keeping a cow bone for every year that passes, upstairs in her attic. The friar and his assistant try to count them but there are so many bones that they get tired of counting and simply agree with The Cailleach that she is very old.

Baba Yaga

Baba Yaga is perhaps the most famous character in Eastern European folklore and she is closely linked to bones – she is one of my favourite ladies in folklore. Baba Yaga lives in a hut with chicken legs. Some stories have described Baba Yaga as a skeletal old woman, showing off her bones, at least partially. Her legs bare, showing her white bones and we can actually find references about her as the bony leg one. Baba Yaga, a character commonly used to scare children in Eastern European literature, is much more than just an evil witch, in fact, I think this is about time we reclaim as a Goddess, because she is a form The Bone Mother In the stories, she is a trickster, yes, but I strongly believe she was devilish because she was powerful and feared. Unfortunately, such an important character as Baba Yaga, who survived for centuries in oral culture, made it into written literature quite far from her original form. When she is first mentioned in a book from 1755, she is no longer the ancient goddess that I believe she is.

Baba Yaga is for some scholars the personification of winter. In Eastern Europe, winter is harsh, wild, dark, dangerous, and also lethal. In this sense, Baba Yaga, Iaga or Jaga, as she is known in different Slavic dialects, is nothing more than a natural force that, when humanised, is feared. Because not even a filter of humanity is enough to hide her wild origin, a storm cannot be sifted. Unfortunately, because of this we find more stories focused on her dark side. Baba Yaga is a supernatural Babushka who knows the medicine of the forest, enchantments and one who prepares potions.

Beyond being the personification of Winter, scholars also believe Baba Yaga to possibly be as I said, The Bone Mother, a deity related to the cult of the dead and the ancestors and in the stories, that connection of the witch of the East with death is still very palpable. In this sense, Baba Yaga, as we find her in the fairytales, would be a psychopomp or a deity in charge of leading souls to the underworld or a guardian of the entrance to the world of the dead. I will go a bit further, because there is a detail that, although small, could also be related to funeral rites. The number of people who end up burned in Baba Yaga's oven, including herself in one of the stories, could be clear examples of cremation. Interesting, isn't it?

Baba Yaga, before taking the human form of the old woman we know, could have been also an animal, possibly a snake or a dragon. This is mentioned in at least one story about how Baba Yaga where she turned into a serpent when she died. Of course, this could also be the influence of the church and the negative connotations with snakes. However, another scholar, Michael Shapiro, relates Baba Yaga to a Paleolithic Bird Goddess, more specifically a Pelican Goddess. Hence her legs are boney and skinny.

Furthermore, we find a close relationship with Baba Yaga and the Amanita muscaria and with Siberia. Shapiro managed to etymologically relate the origin of the word Yaga with the Samoyed peoples of Siberia and highlighted the possible cultural contacts between Slavs and these tribes. If Baba Yaga has a Siberian origin, we could perfectly explain the importance of the amanita muscaria in her folklore, because there are people who see Yaga as the spirit of the amanita itself. If she is Siberian, it would also explain why the witch can smell the Russians and is even a bit hostile towards them. If she is a Samoyed, she is a Tribal Goddess, a shaman, she is a foreigner.

As we can see, Yaga is a complex character. In the stories, we are presented with Baba Yaga as an evil and dangerous old woman who goes out to hunt children or who kills people who are lost in the forest. She devours their flesh and decorated her fence made of bones with their skulls. An evil witch, long feared by superstitious peasants. This terrible image of the Baba Yaga we know comes to us from the Middle Ages. The church is guilty of demonising the wise, old woman of the forest, to frighten the parishioners and their children. She is a key piece of popular folklore from the East. But Yaga is also somehow the living flame of an ancient deity, who would have survived shapeshifting over the millennia, within Baba Yaga, remaining hidden under all the layers and concepts and stories about the witch.

The spirit of this prehistoric deity, The Bone Mother, of my dear Baba Yaga, does not remain contained in Eastern Europe. We find the traces of the witch travelling west, transforming along the way, taking on new identities, just as many other deities have. We can find traces of her in the Iron Woman or the Woman with the Iron Nose in Ukrainian folklore, also Hungarians have an Iron Nose woman. We also find Yaga in Ježibaba or Baba Pehtra in Slovakia, in Dokia in Romania, and in Worawy in West Germany. The Wjera and Iron Tooth Woman of the Sorbian people would be an analogue of Baba Yaga and the Bulgarian Lamia also somehow substitutes the witch in the stories. Here we also find Baba Yaga's relationship with serpent deities so this shouldn't come as a surprise. Plus, the Bulgarian Forest Mother would also be an analogue of the witch and we find Mother Forestas as a common figure in other countries in the area. In German-speaking countries we find analogues of the witch under the names Holda or Frau Holle, Frau Hulle, Holla,

Holda, Chlungery, Perchta, Domina Perchta, Berchta, Berta and Bertha, in the alpine regions and towards the North. To the south, in France, we find the figure of "La Reine Pédauque" which would be translated as the Queen of Goose Legs, another clear reference to the Bird Goddess and as I already mentioned, she is closely related to the Iberian Goddess, The Cailleach. Yes, you read that right! The Cailleach is another form of the Bone Mother. But we also find in North Africa references to an Ogre with huge breasts that she has to throw over her shoulders to jump from one place to the other. Cailleach is also an Ogre Goddess and we know that she travelled great distances so, maybe she crossed the Strait of Gibraltar, just as she crossed the sea towards Ireland and later Scotland, even further North to Scandinavia. I believe Baba Yaga could be the other great Goddess that conquered Europe, along with Astarte, only we have failed to recognize her importance until now.

Hecate

Perhaps one of the goddesses about which there is more information available right now is the Goddess Hecate. For this reason, I am just going to explore here in brief her relationship to bones. If you want to explore the Goddess of the Crossroads, I would recommend reading; *Hekate Soteira* by Sarah Iles Johnston, *Hekate Liminal Rites and the Circle for Hekate volume I*, by Sorita d'Este, or the *Chaldean Oracles*. Although we find Hecate integrated and with a relevant role in the Greek pantheon, the reality is that Hecate could be a much older Goddess. Some scholars look to ancient Thrace as the possible origin of Hecate but we can also move on the map towards the Near East, to ancient Mesopotamia, to find the possible origin of Hecate.

Various excavations at crossroads have brought to light deposits of dog bones, both adults and puppies. The crossroads are places linked to the Goddess Hecate, one of her epithets is

Trivia (of the three paths), and we know people placed offerings for her in these places. We also know about the use of puppies in healing processes in antiquity and Hecate is a matron goddess, linked to childbirth. We find her depicted together with dogs in several classical images. Some of animal bones found, would be linked to offerings, as well as to magical and ritual practices. We know the practice of sacrificing dogs to Hecate as part of funeral rites would have been common. Statues have also been found representing Hecate with the head of a dog and there was also the common practice of eating dog to honour Hecate.

Kankala Murti

Kankala Murti or Gangalamurti is a destructive aspect of Lord Shiva. We find Kalanka Murti dancing, carrying bones and skulls of various animals, not just humans. He is, so to speak, a bearer of the truth of all that he inhabits, so the bones would represent the truth behind outward appearances.

This aspect of Shiva is especially feared as he has the power to destroy the world when the purpose of existence deviates from the truth and goes the wrong way. In addition to being a destroyer of demons and evil in general. Perhaps because of his immense power and despite being an aspect or emanation of Shiva, he does not have too many devotees. On the contrary, it seems to me an ideal deity to undo or destroy the veils of illusion of Maya and bring the truth to the surface when necessary.

Bau

Goddess Bau, known as Gula in Babylon, was a daughter of Anu, King of Heavens and ruling King of the ancient Gods of the Sumerian Pantheon. She was the wife of Ninurta and one of the most important Goddesses of the Sumerians. Bau was possibly a Creation Mother Goddess in origin, matron of Lagash. With time, she evolved to become a healing Goddess, most likely due to her association with the dogs and their own association with healing. Dogs were supposed to be healers, licking wounds and dressing them. Such is Bau's relationship with dogs that she was sometimes represented with a dog's head.

Bau is a goddess of labour and childbirth, she could be related to fertility or even abundance. She is called Beneficent Protective Goddess but it is her healing role that has endured through the millennia. Bau was not just a mere healing goddess, she was the Supreme Healer. As her sacred animal, dogs were cared for in her temples and by her devotees. Dogs were not only part of the healing process and healing related rituals, dogs were also sacrificed to Bau, as is deduced from the remains of dog bones that have been found buried in her temples.

Bau is still a relevant Goddess today. Perhaps there is a renewed curiosity towards her, especially for the devotees of the Goddess Hecate, since Bau is seen as the possible origin deity of Goddess of the Crossroads. The Titan Goddess, would be the result of Bau's journey and her emanation to the Balkans and ancient Greece. This theory is not so far-fetched, since Bau/Hecate would not be the only Mesopotamian Goddess to gain a foothold in the Greek pantheon. Bau would also be related to the Goddess Baubo.

Kali

When we find ourselves before Kali, we can't help but feel intimidated, at least at first.

Kali glares at us, eyes wide, her red tongue sticking out of her. Hanging from the neck, a garland of human heads and I have also seen this garland made of skulls. Sometimes she holds n her hands, a sword, a sacrificial ceremonial knife and other weapons, she also holds the head of a demon. This simple image is enough to terrify the neophyte or those unaware of this goddess. Kali is considered the consort of Shiva. I am personally inclined to believe that Kali could be an emanation of Parvati and I have read other people expressing this. This would make total sense, Kali being the consort of Shiva and Kankala Murti being one of his emanations. Both Kali and Kankala Murti have in this sense a similar vibration. If we place Kali and Kankala Murti side by side, perhaps we will have a little more clarity regarding the nature of their relationship. She is Death, he is the skeleton. But they share more than just bones in their representations, they do vibrate similar, energy wise.

Kali is death, but she kills demons, the death that she brings, could well be the death of the ego. She sticks her tongue out at us, challenges us, she tries to scare us. The gesture of sticking the tongue out in an intimidating way is also found in the Egyptian God Bes. Maori also stick out their tongues while performing a Haka maybe for the same reasons.

We are in front of a destroyer of illusion, falsehood, ego and maya in general. She is change, chaos, the almighty force that destroys what does not help us in our purpose. She helps us deal with and kill our personal demons and destroys obstacles in our way. Devotees usually pray to the goddess with a mala made of bone carved in the shape of skulls.

Priapus

Considered a lesser god of the Greek pantheon, Priapus, son of Aphrodite, cursed by the envious Hera with a huge erect phallus, is expelled from Olympus for being considered grotesque, to the point that his own mother disregards him. He was associated with fertility, livestock, gardens, crops, fruits and of course, with sexuality and male genitalia. Curiously, he is also related to merchant sailors.

In Greece, after his exile from Olympus, Priapus becomes a God of rural character, with humble devotees — shepherds and farmers. Although no great temples were erected to Priapus for this reason, we do know that donkeys were sacrificed to him. Legend has it that finding Hestia asleep, Priapus tries to rape her and a donkey alerts the Goddess, waking her up. But that would not be the only reason why Priapus would hate donkeys. Another story tells how a donkey challenges him to see who has the biggest phallus. Priapus would win the challenge and kill the donkey as payment for the insult, as shown by the donkey bones that have been found in places related to the god. In the Museum of Naples there is a relief found in a garden of a Roman villa in Capri. In the relief we see Priapus represented riding on top of a donkey.

In addition to his relationship with agriculture, Priapus was represented in gardens and different figures of the god have been found. Priapus, in a way, became the first garden gnome in history. Being a minor deity, we find that Priapus was often honoured alongside other gods, such as Dionysus, with whom he is closely related, as well as the god Pan. Despite not being the typical god, we find that Priapus had a fairly widespread cult and that it reached distant places in the empire. Mentions of Priapus have been found, for example, in the north of England and Scotland. Hera somehow failed in her curse and Priapus endured.

Prometheus the Titan

We have already reviewed the story of how Prometheus tricked Zeus and offered him bones, but who was he? A second-generation Titan, Prometheus is the grandson of Uranus and Gaia, the son of Iapetus, and the brother of Atlas, Epimetheus, and Menoetius. Prometheus is popularly known as a God of fire, for having stolen the fire of the Gods for men. But Prometheus is also a creator God who is credited with creating humans from clay and water.

Although Prometheus supports Zeus in the war against the Titans, he offends him and is punished for it. The God Hephaestus is in charge of chaining him to the mountain with adamantium chains, following orders from Zeus. During his thousand-year sentence, Prometheus is visited by various deities, some offering help, such as the Titan, Oceanus and the Nymph, Io. Even Hermes visits him, to ask for information for Zeus but Prometheus refuses to collaborate with Hermes, who mocks Prometheus and his luck and gives him up for lost. Prometheus's pain only ends when he is freed by the hero Melqart/Hercules.

Mictlāntēcutli

Aztec God of the Kingdom of the Dead, the Skeleton God who together with his wife, Mictecacihuatl, Goddess of Death, governed the Mictlan. Though in reality the role of Mictlāntēcutli in the daily spirituality of the Aztecs went beyond being the God of Death. He also represented rebirth and fertility, both of men and of the fields. It was the Spanish chroniclers who superimposed more information to his role as God of the underworld. Perhaps impressed by the sacrifices to God, this idea contributed to Mictlāntēcutli being compared to the devil.

Hispanic chronicles speak of human sacrifices and ritual anthropophagy in the last month of the Rainy Season, Tititl. At the end of the Dry Season, Mictlāntēcutli was honoured and the Dead were celebrated. On those dates, according to the chronicles, a representative was chosen in the Land of God, an older man who was adorned with jewels and well dressed. They would then lock him in, sealing the door and leaving him inside with a limited amount of food. The intention was that the man would starve, that his body would be consumed and that he would become a skeleton, to resemble Mictlāntēcutli.

The Spanish chroniclers left us a rather dark image of the God. But they were people outside the cult who did not understand what they were seeing, they also had a strong demonising filter. They focussed on the parts which they saw as inhuman, diabolical. The mere fact of witnessing how the statue of Mictlāntēcutli was bathed in the blood of the sacrificed, was enough for them to classify him as a god of death.

In Codex Tudela, we find the testimony of how some people made blood offerings to the god. They went to the temple and punctured their tongues, ears, wrists, thighs and other parts of the body, they bled to offer their blood. This was collected by the priest and was poured on the head of the statue of the god, to ask for health or for the deceased who were already in Mictlan, the kingdom of Mictlāntēcutli.

But it was not just the blood that would also have left a strong impression among the Spaniards, but the fact that bones and skulls were deposited at the feet of the statue as well. These are not the only bones that we find in relation to Mictlāntēcutli — he is guardian of the bones of the first inhabitants of the world and the first gods.

Hel

Hel, one of Loki's three children with the giantess Angrboda. Her name means 'Hidden' in Old Norse and Hel ruled over the underworld which was known by the same name that she bore. The first mentions of Hel are found in the Skaldic Verses, Ragnarsdrápa, which are said to have been written prior to the year 900.

As the story goes, once the existence of Hel and her brothers, the Serpent Jörmungandr and the Wolf Fenrir, is discovered, Odin has them brought before him. He appoints Hel to the underworld. The kingdom of Hel, would be, according to some sources, the prelude to the kingdom of Niflheim, mainly due to the references to the Kingdom of Hel as a hall or a room.

We do not find much information about Hel in the Eddas, where she is mentioned superficially. Only in the Myth about the Death of Baldur, can we read something more about her.

What is mentioned about Hel does not leave us with a very friendly image of the Goddess. She is the personification of Death. She is described as cold, cruel, with no empathy for the souls that come to her realm or for the inhabitants of the other realms.

With her blue skin, perhaps due to the cold at the gates of Niflheim, she shows her flesh and bones. Some descriptions describe her as having a perpetual smile, perhaps because part of her jaw is visible. Hel is a giant, let's not forget that her mother was a giant too.

It is also mentioned that Hel is related to the horses — such references have been found from the 9th century.

Astarte

The Canaanite — Phoenician Goddess Astarte, is perhaps one of the most complex Goddesses of antiquity. Her cult did not disappear completely, since under other names and guises, traces of the cult of the Goddess have survived to this day, even syncretized in figures of the Catholic cult in the Mediterranean, but she made it as far as the British Islands, as we know for the archeological evidence found here. There are several shrines dedicated to Astarte, Dea Caelestis and the Syrian Goddess along Hadrian's Wall and Scotland. I have seen them in the local museums. Astarte was known as Ishtar to the Akkadians and possibly a form of Inanna to the Sumerians. She appears in the Old Testament as Astarot or Celestial Goddess. She is Dea Caelestis and possibly the origin of other Goddesses, such as Aphrodite-Venus, Tanit, Hathor or even Isis and Nut with whom she is closely related to. She is the Highest Goddess, the one in the highest place. We may even find in Astarte, the origin of the Celtic Goddess Brigantia and the clues to this relationship are found in Iberia and the epithets Turobriga and Turobrigensis. There was also the city of Brigantia, the modern A Coruña, in Galicia.

She is the Marine Goddess par excellence, protector of sailors and fishermen. She conquered the ancient world at the hands of the Phoenicians and clearly crossed the borders of the Mediterranean. We could very well find in Astarte the origin of Germanic and Celtic Goddesses, even Norse deities. Goddess of War and Goddess of Fertility — there are few Goddesses as charismatic as Astarte. Perhaps because of the Goddess being so rich in her attributes and qualities, it was easier for her to give rise to so many other Goddesses. In Greece, she is believed to be the origin not only of Aphrodite, but of Athena and Diana — she is even related to Artemis. Her emanations are still worshipped by many modern pagan practitioners, even if they ignore the real origin of their Goddesses. In a way she lives through all of her emanations. She has endured, for millennia.

As it happens with Bau or Hecate, bone remains of the sacrifice of dogs have been found in places related to her cult, but also of equines. Sometimes represented as the consort of Melqart, we cannot exclude that human sacrifices were also made to her, more so as she was such an important Goddess. We know that this was the case with Melqart or with the God, Baal, who also appears to be linked to Astarte.

Triton

Sea god of Greek mythology, Triton, has a semi-human appearance. He has the tail of a fish and the torso of a man, what we would call a merman. He is the son of the God of Poseidon and the Goddess of the Sea Amphitrite. Although, according to Homer, Triton's house under the sea was in the Aegean Sea, we also find him linked to Libya and a salt lake that bears his name.

According to mythology, Triton has a Conch Trumpet thought to be magical in nature. When he touches her, he can calm sea waters or produce large waves or even storms. Triton is represented with one or two tails and it is said that he was like a kind of messenger for his father — he was in charge of announcing his presence. Being the son of Poseidon, we see Triton carrying the Trumpet Shell, he is rarely depicted with a trident.

Triton is given the paternity of minor deities called Tritones, something like mermen, although sometimes instead of a fish tail, they have been represented with half the body of a crab or lobster. Tritones have a violent and temperamental nature. Somehow, they represent the darkest side of the nature of their grandfather Poseidon. We could say that Poseidon's divine essence is diluted each generation and also each generation grows further from humanity. Pausanias, a Greek traveller and geographer, described them as grotesque-looking beings, with greenish skin and misshapen features. They are sometimes accused of assaulting women who went to the beach alone.

Chapter 5

Bones and Living Traditions

In this journey through the world of bones we have reached a special place. We are going to review the use of bones not only in traditions that remained in antiquity, but that are still alive in some way. For example, hoodoo or voodoo or necromancy are not dead traditions, far from it! The cult of ancestors is also alive in many places! There are many people out there who still use bones in their spiritual practices. Of course, some of these practices unfortunately have to go through the filter of the new age. Some magical practitioners criticise and refuse to be associated with practitioners that work with bones or other animal parts such as furs. It is a personal choice but there are many people who are still connected with the bones and with the ancestors and should be left in peace to practice as we choose. We should be mindful and respect that differing opinions exist.

One of my intentions with this book is to give the bones a voice — to somehow speak of them with pride, as an important part of us and our history. In this part of the book, I also give voice to modern practitioners who are connected to the bones. Indigenous people, rootworkers, necromancers, shamans, druids and foragers that roam the forests. There are many of us who are united by the bones. It is truly beautiful to encounter these connections.

A Dress Made of Bones

Cave paintings show us the interaction of humans with different animals, carrying their bones and skins. The Wizards of the rois-Frères cave in Montesquieu-Avantès, Ariège, France and the shamans in the Caves of Tamgaly, Siberia. The paintings tell us stories of hunts, rituals and magic.

The use of regalia with animal parts is not limited to a specific place, since they are used by different indigenous groups in different latitudes: shamans in Siberia, witches, healers, medicine people, spirit people in Africa, the Amazon Jungles, the Plains of North America, Japan. Even if you don't know much about animism or shamanism, if someone asks you what a shaman looks like, the image that comes to mind is of a person wearing a headdress with the horns of some animal, maybe even part of the head and skins or feathers. It could also be that they carried shells or small bones in their hair as beads, maybe even seeds.

It is not only the spirit people that wear regalia (these are special outfits that are worn on occasions with a marked importance). There are peoples that use their regalia for rites of passage, for meetings or festivals. We cannot confuse wearing regalia with dressing up. These outfits have a very marked spiritual character and the elements used usually have an important meaning for those societies.

Even today, there are peoples in the arctic circle that still dress with furs, just as our hunter-gatherer ancestors did. We are so immersed in our modern society that it is hard for us to imagine that there are still people on this planet who live outside the system. Living in the same way that their ancestors did, from mother earth, in harmony with their space and understanding their resources. When we need clothes and food, we go shopping. They went out to hunt and used every part of the animal; its meat to eat, its bones to create tools (such as sewing needles, scrapers to clean the skins) and its skin to make their clothes, to create their homes, blankets, etc.

Perhaps you have seen some breastplates made of bones. These were not merely decorative; the bone is a hard material worn on the chest or neck in the form of a choker for protection. If you get shot with an arrow in the chest, the breastplates made for rudimentary armour. If you wear a choker and someone tries to cut your throat, it is already something between your skin and the blade. Traditionally these were made with bird bones although bear and even wolf bones are also used.

Necromancy

Between the first ceremonies around death by Neanderthals and the most complex religious beliefs is where the underworld takes on an important role. Beliefs from which we also see the emergence of a multitude of Chthonic Deities in various geographies. At some point in that line, the need arose to communicate with the dead and establish a communication bridge with the underworld or the other side of the veil. And of course, when that need is created, the figure of the necromancer appears, as a facilitator of that communication between the dead and the living.

Perhaps in the shamans of prehistory and their successors in animistic cultures, we find the oldest necromancers in history. The manipulation of skulls is seen in different archaeological sites of the Neolithic era, not only the pigmentation of the skulls. The attempted reconstruction of the features of the deceased, even using shells to replace the eyes and facial recreations, gives rise to many speculations and theories, but it tells us in some way of the magical use of these skulls.

Although the practice of necromancy emerged with the Cult of the Ancestors, the origin of the word necromancy is found in Greece, νεκρομαντεία (nekromanteía). This is a word composed of nekrós — νεκρός, dead, corpse and manteía — μαντεία and that translates as divination. Although it is not in Greece where we find the origin of these practices, there we find philosophers who were called shamans who were said to be necromancers. Among them, Pythagoras, Aristeas, Epimenides or Hermotimus. Of these names, perhaps you are familiar with Pythagoras, who was closely related to necromancy and was said to have learned the necromantic arts in Persia, although some scholars have found connections between Pythagoras and Orphism, and it is even speculated that Pythagoras had been initiated into the Orphic Mysteries.

In addition to the famous story of Orpheus and Eurydice described by Plato, we find necromantic Practices in other examples of Greek literature, such as Homer's Odyssey. In the aforementioned text we find how Odysseus seeks Circe's help to perform a ritual not only to appease one of his deceased men whom they did not help, but also to cut off the heads of several sheep and offer their blood to the deceased. Also, the hero Aeneas with the help of the Sibyl, is launched in search of the entrance to the underworld to find his father.

One of Pythagoras students, Empedocles, would also have been classified as a necromancer. But perhaps the most curious relationship with necromancy is found in Epimenides. Not only do we know that he exorcised the city of Athens and freed it of ghosts, but that he continued to somehow offer prophecies after his death, since a part of his skin that was tattooed was used as an oracle.

But this fact should not surprise us, since there is knowledge of the use of skulls or human heads for prophecy by different necromancers. Legend has it that the head of Orpheus himself ended up in a cave on the island of Lesbos, after being dismembered by the women of his tribe and that the head would have continued to give prophecies to anyone who visited.

Perhaps linked to the belief that after death a new door to knowledge or higher knowledge opens, we could find one of the reasons for the emergence of necromancy. Necromancers in Babylon, called Manzuzuu or Sha'etemmu, were regularly consulted by kings who based important decisions on their predictions. Apart from the magical and oracular factor in the works of necromancy, of course, we could also talk about an emotional factor involved in the practice of necromancy.

My first experiences using a ouija board were with my father when I was very young, around five years old, because he wanted to communicate with his deceased mother. A practice that he performed in private, hidden from the eyes of strangers. Part of the darkness that surrounds the necromantic practices in some way could also be related to the obscurantism that surrounds the rituals, which were kept secret or away from the public gaze.

In summary, we could group the uses of necromancy into two branches:

- Sympathetic necromancy: Where the person who practises has an emotional bond with the deceased and uses the necromancer techniques to reconnect with the soul of the person.
- Beneficial necromancy: Where the person who practises calls any spirit with the sole intention of gathering knowledge for personal benefit.

With regards to where necromancy was performed, I have already mentioned that it was something that was practised secretly, so it should not surprise us to find oracles who spoke with the dead in caves. Perhaps for direct access to the underworld such locations facilitated the journey of the person to the deceased as necromantic practices tried to bring the dead to the world of the living or the living person had to approach the world of the dead. A cavern is a perfect place to approach the world of the dead.

In *The Odyssey*, Circe instructs Odysseus to dig a hole in the ground to pour his offerings to the dead. This act of digging is a very clear change of level, in an attempt to approach those who are underground. In fact, those of us who are familiar with shamanic work carry out this change of level, from one reality to another, journeying between worlds. We move to the worlds below or to the underworld just as a necromancer would to speak with the dead, the ancestors. But these practices are not something modern or new, since the "Greek Shamans", who arise from the teachings of the Pythagorean School, also naturally incorporated necromancy into their practices.

Another of the usual places for necromancy practices would be tombs. The necromancer would visit the tomb, the last resting place of the dead. Despite the years passed, there are relatives who visit the remains of their dead ones in cemeteries, bring them flowers, pray to them and celebrate them because they believe that there is a connection with the person in that very place. There are still people who believe that the deceased are tied to their bones and that their soul would wander not too far from them. Based on this belief the necromancer goes to graves in search of souls to consult. Although it is also worth mentioning the practice of evoking the spirit of a dead person next to their statue. A practice that varies very little from that of invoking the gods next to their statues. The statue would act as a vehicle for the soul of the person, since it would be representing a likeness of that person.

Another good place to find souls would have been the battlefields. For obvious reasons, these would have been perhaps the easiest place to find wandering souls, due to the violent nature of the deaths. It is highly possible that more than one soul would have been trapped in such a place, linked to their bones. Even more so if their remains had not been honoured after the battle or had simply been abandoned out in the open. In the necromantic practices on the battlefields, the remains of heroes would have been especially valued.

Basic elements or technologies within necromantic practices:

1. Purification – Perhaps one of the most important parts of the pre-consultation preparations. Sometimes those purifications would have started up to 21 days before it.

2. Consultation time – The time chosen for the practice used to fall at night, as it was the hours of darkness when the ghosts would wander.

3. Pit and Fire – As a focal centre of the rite. The pit to offer the libations and blood, and the fire to burn the remains of the sacrifice.

4. Libations – These had to have the quality of infusing life. For example, the Melikraton, a mixture of Milk and Honey that used to be given to new-borns. As the first food of the living, it was a perfect option for the dead. There would also be sweet wine, water and cereals such as oatmeal.

5. Sacrifice and Blood – The animal sacrifices would have included one or two black rams. Although we find mention of the sacrifice of black bulls or black Heifers. The blood would have been offered in the pit for the dead. Jason, instructed by Medea, in practices classified as highly necromantic, invokes Hecate by sacrificing three black dogs.

6. Prayers and Incantations – An important part of the rite would have been the act of vocally expressing the magic words, incantations or prayers. We find several examples of utterances in the different Greco-Egyptian Magical Papyri.

7. Movement – Not just the circular movement around the focal points, for example, the circular libations in the pit. There are also mentions of jumping as part of the common movements and we cannot rule out that gestures were used as part of a sacred drama during the rite.

8. Management or the Spirit – The technologies for the management of the spirit would have been subject mainly to their reaction to the call. Since either it would have been the case that the spirit was eager to speak or on the contrary, that it was reluctant to share information. Another point to take into account would

have been knowing how to repel unwanted spirits, since blood offerings could attract others, not just the one who was invoked. Technologies to keep the summoned spirit in the service of the summoner and prevent it from returning to the spirit world would also have been very important. We also find mention in the Magical Papyri the act of dismissing the spirit after completing the work.

9. Bowls – There are several mentions of the use of bowls in divinatory practices. Different substances would have been poured into them to propitiate a reading, which would preferably have been carried out by young boys.

10. Dolls or statues – The use of wax dolls had already been found in ancient Mesopotamia and this practice would have continued in Greece as well. Wax, due to its plastic qualities, would have been an ideal technology to create dolls, as well as clay. The use of dolls and statues would have been similar, as a vehicle of connection with the spirit.

11. Rings – We find in the Greek Magical Papyri, the mention of a ring that, among other qualities, could facilitate the invocation of ghosts and spirits to whoever wore it. Although in reality what would have given the ring such qualities would have been the stone it contained, a heliotrope.

12. Etiquette in necromancy – Although we automatically turn to black, as the main colour of the necromancer's clothes, we find that, for example, Odysseus is pre-presented naked during his practices. Various protective amulets could also have been included as part of the regalia.

Bones in Magical Grimoires

Bones, necromancy, magic, angels and demons — we find magical uses or rituals with bones in different grimoires of antiquity. From the Greek Magical Papyri of the 2nd century BCE, through the Testament of Solomon, 2nd or 3rd century, the Sword of Moses from the 8th or 10th century, Picatrix from the 10th century, Sepher Raziel from the year 1259, Hygromanteia from the year 1440, to a total of 28 Grimoires that contain something related to bones.

Of course, these were popular beliefs and we can clearly see how some of these uses are related to the qualities of the animal or person the bone came from. We could say that somehow it was sympathetic magic, with animistic touches. These uses are recorded in the aforementioned grimoires. The inclusion of this data is purely informative in relation to past practices.

Animal bones

Dog bones used to be credited with healing properties, although if the dog was black, it also helped you gain invisibility. The bone of a black cat also made you invisible. Frog bones seemed to be popular, either they helped you attract the desired person to your bed, or they helped you get sex. In contrast, ground pork bones would help nullify sexual desire. Bones from a donkey's back helped you get a woman and donkey bones would have been used in spells to reduce someone's intelligence.

Lion bones had been used for rituals to gain strength and the wing bones of certain birds had been used to silence gossip and make a sharp-tongued person suffer. The bones of a Civet would serve to make everyone hate a person and the bones of rabbits or hares would serve to get rid of a love rival.

Human bones

A couple of uses of children's bones are found in the *Book of Saint Cyprian*. The left femur bone of a child under 6 months would help you dissolve an unwanted marriage and the bone of a child would also be used for divination. Moving to adult bones, seven honey-roasted bones would have been used to guess someone's intentions during a storm and two bones were used to speak with the dead, while a single bone helped to utter a curse.

Sometimes healing properties were attributed to human bones. We find that in three grimoires, *Grand Albert* of the year 1493, the *Discoverie of Witchcraft* of the year 1584 and *Egyptian Secrets of Albertus Magnus* of the year 1725 mentions are made of the use of human bones to cure or create charms against epilepsy. Bone powder would also be used to cure cancer or to control bleeding. Bone scraped from the inside of a skull was thought to remedy gout.

The skulls had very varied uses. The skull of a thief could help you recover stolen goods, also the skull of a criminal served as a cure for rabies. They were also used for divination (to be able to dominate a spirit, to do good or evil) and to get invisibility or more intelligence. Also, to cause harm to another person, as well as to make the crop grow.

Autumn Stormcaller and Her Bones

Autumn Stormcaller is a member of the Mesa Grande Kumeyaay Tribe in California. Her relationship with the bones is something traditional and personal at the same time. When she was a child, during walks in the forest, her grandparents would teach her the love of looking for bones, animal remains and crystals. the love of looking for bones, animal remains and crystals. Along with her father and her brother, she grew up hunting for bones on a regular basis.

As many natives do, she also rescues carcasses of animals killed on the road and she learned to honour them. She shows respect to the animal's spirit by moving it off the road to prevent it from being hit again. Sometimes those animals are buried, other times she takes part of the animal back to her home, to clean the bones and honour them. With the bones she sometimes makes jewellery or simply leaves them on display. But she doesn't take every bone she finds. There are bones or remains that it is better to leave where they were found, the spirit may not want to be disturbed or the bones are somehow already part of the ground.

The struggle of her tribe to recover ancestral lands goes beyond territorial or political reasons. Of course, the government should return those lands that were unfairly taken from them but, for the tribe it is also important to be able to recover the remains of their ancestors, to be able to honour them. Autumn Stormcaller's tribe is working to open a museum/cultural centre, to honour their people and to share knowledge about their heritage with respect.

Greywolf: A Druid and His Bones

Philip Shallcrass, Greywolf, is the Chief Druid of the British Druid Order. Although I have found during my research that not all druids work with bones, many make an animistic connection to the animal through the bones. This is not an isolated phenomenon within druidry, especially among druids who reside in a rural setting who tend to at least collect the bones they find to honour the spirit of the animal.

Greywolf shares with me his story, how his first contact with bones occurred in the 70s, when he bought a human skull, although at that point, he confesses that apart from its decorative use, he never worked with it on a magical level. Partly out of respect, since it didn't seem right to him.

Working with bones began shortly after encountering a wolf spirit from whom he received his craft name, Greywolf. A gift, a wolf tooth that was sent by a friend in the Pacific Northwest of the USA. He wore it as a pendant for some years until he lost it one day, in the London streets on New Year's Day, 2000. But he is sure that this loss was a payment to the spirit of the wolf for helping him temporarily heal his wife, who was very sick.

But that was not the end of Greywolf's story with the spirit of the Wolf, as another gift arrived, a wolf-skin cloak made from the hides of six wolves. Working with it, and with wolf spirit, took away the last vestiges of his concerns about working with animal parts.

Greywolf shares:

My wolves, and my wolf alter ego, not surprisingly love venison. This led me to work with deer. An antler from a white roebuck taught me a deer chant I sometimes use in ceremonies. I also started making frame drums, the frames from ash trees and the skins from red deer hides obtained from an annual cull undertaken at a deer park to keep numbers down to what the land can sustain in the absence of other-than-human predators. Some of the drums have handles made from red deer leg bones.

I also make flutes from red deer leg bones. These have been made in the British Isles for millennia. The first one I made is a little three-holed one based on a sketch of a now lost original found in a Bronze Age burial mound near Avebury, not far from where I live. I've played it at Avebury, which gives a particularly strong sense of communing with the ancestors there. The deer bones used primarily come from butchers who would otherwise bin them.

Playing the drums or flutes gives a strong sense of connection with the animal people from whom they are made, both the individual animals and the spirit of the species. This is simultaneous with the sense of connecting with ancestors who made and played similar instruments in the past. This is enhanced by playing them in ceremonial settings. For specifically honouring deer spirit in ceremony, I have a tabard made from the hide of a large red deer to which deer bones are attached that produce clattering chimes when I move. For me, connecting and communing with the spirits of animal people and human ancestors is a strong part of what druidry is and what gives it its power.

Having worked with bones and other animal parts as part for some years now, in his Druidic Path, Greywolf has come to an understanding that the bones retain at least a part of the spirit of the animal person they come from, and that those animal people are often happy to work with us. Through the music and the ceremonies in which they are used, there is a renewing or enhancing their connection with this world. They, their energy, live again in our world, dancing, speaking and singing with us through drums, flutes, rattles...

Greywolf continues to share and makes a very interesting and truthful point:

A few centuries ago, when most of us were actively engaged in agriculture and relied on horses for transport, working with animal parts would be regarded as a normal part of life. Now we are mostly removed from the lives of animals other than pets. We are also removed from human death by medical professionals and undertakers. In the absence of a visceral relationship with the deaths of either animals or humans, many of us come to regard bones and other animal parts as somehow sinister. The widespread lack of belief in a life beyond physical death, other than possibly as ghosts or revenants in horror stories, adds to the sense that working with animal parts is wrong. Like most things in life, it depends on how you approach it. If you have empathy for the dead and are willing to listen to them, such work can be richly rewarding for all concerned.

The Druid of Chiltern Hills and His Bone House

In the northwest of London there is a place of singular beauty that stretches across several counties. The Druid of Chiltern Hill grew up among woods and the hills of flint and chalk. He and the other children always found bones of badgers, hares, deer rabbits and foxes everywhere. They were the hills of bones! He tells me how his grandfather used to hang deer skulls around his cherry orchard. He also hung the skulls with wire from the trees, as if it were a kind of warning to the deer themselves, so that they would not approach the trees and their tender shoots. He grew up among bones and feathers and found them absolutely magical — special, different. Somehow, they were sacred, treasures that were later shown to others as relics that later ended up on altars or placed onto trees. Over the years and his forays into magic, he would later be initiated as a druid, the bones have been an important part of his path and many times he returned to the hills to celebrate the spirit of animals in a ritual way. In his exploration of working with bones, he has created magical tools with them, musical instruments and has also used them for divination. He uses animal horns to create instruments such as trumpets and drinking vessels. He also carves them, creating his own scrimshaw.

Over the years, he built a roundhouse that he calls the Bone House, dedicated to animal spirits, to honour them. He has not only deposited bones there that he has found locally, but also those found on his travels. There are people who also bring bones that they find. It is a magical and special place, to connect with the spirits, although not all the bones there are from animals. He sourced some human bones through a doctor, and came to create a flute with one of them. Somehow those human bones create a balance, they make it clear that we are all the same and that we will all end up being that, bones, all of us being vertebrates.

But the Bone House is not the only special place that this druid guards. Not far from him, there is a tree that he calls Grandmother Elder to which he usually takes the remains of animals from his hunts or road kills, so that they somehow feed Grandmother Elder with their flesh and blood, as offerings. But taking the animal to her is also a healing act, post mortem, especially for those animals that have died after being hit by a car. He takes them to Grandmother Elder to give them peace and help them cross over to the other side. This I find beautiful and I have done something similar myself, placing animals I found by an ancient tree, using the tree as a portal to the world of the dead too.

This druid follows a path of reconnection with ancient customs and technologies. He learned to use all parts of the animal, with respect and in connection with their spirit. A path that keeps him away from computers and telephones for several days, more in connection with nature.

Eagle Bone Whistle

The Lakota people and other native peoples of North America use a whistle made from eagle bone. This is not to be mistaken for a musical instrument. The Eagle Bone Whistle is a ritual instrument that is used in different ceremonies, including the Sun Dance. The person who is Sun Dancing should be blowing his whistle while in the dance area. By doing this you breathe faster, you are altering your breath with each step.

The act of taking a rapid breath while whistling, would induce an altered state of consciousness. Add to this that as a Sun Dancer, you are in a sacred ceremony, sacred space, where drums are being played and sacred songs are being sung. These whistles are made religiously and ritually for a sacred purpose.

Kotsuage: A Japanese Funeral Rite

There are few countries in the world with the ritual structure that Japan has. The Japanese live immersed in ritual and ceremony which is integrated into their day-to-day life. We have all heard of the tea ceremony, for example. Knowing that the life of the average Japanese is marked by structure and ceremony, it should not surprise us that their festivities and celebrations are something exceptional. Of course, their funeral rites are not far behind.

Kotsuage is a custom that has its roots in the Shinto Religion, the Way of Kami. Shinto is known as the set of beliefs and practices within Japanese folklore, heir to local animist practices. We cannot forget that an indigenous people still reside within Japanese territory: the Ainu, descendants of the Jōmon Tribes of Hokkaido and the Upper Palaeolithic people of Eurasia.

Despite the efforts of the Japanese government throughout the 19th and 20th century to "convert" the Ainu into Japanese, they almost miraculously survived the acculturation imposed by Japanese forces and armies. Once the government of Japan began annexation of the Ainu territory, this group residing on the island of Hokkaido and other northern territories, not only lost its status as an indigenous people, their numbers greatly reduced during these years of acculturation. The Ainu practices were ridiculed and as happened to indigenous groups in North America, their customs were penalised by the government.

Japan currently has two main religions. Shinto, which predates historical records and Buddhism which entered the country around the 6th century CE. The Ainu were not able to resume their religious practices and their status as an indigenous people until 2008, when the Government returned their status, pushed by the Declaration on the Rights of Indigenous Peoples of 2007. This comes after years of promoting a unique Japanese identity and the Ainu have almost disappeared under pressure from the government and society. Until then, being Ainu or descendants of the Ainu was seen as something dirty. Which pushed many Ainu to completely abandon their identity, often by force, although others would hide their origin in order to integrate with the Japanese. For that reason, although the number of people registered as Ainu is relatively small, it is estimated that there are more descendants of the tribe living in Japan.

Shintoism and Buddhism being the most popular religions, have even complemented each other within the practices of the same family, which would use rituals of one or another tradition for different occasions. The religiosity of the average Japanese revolves around rites of passage, such as births or marriages, and of course, also funeral rites and ancestor worship.

The Kotsuage is an exponent of this syncretization between Shinto and Buddhism and the Cult of the Ancestors. Within the institutionalisation of the funerary practices during the Meiji period, in the Kotsuage the family of the deceased continues to have an important role. They are not only present when the burning proceeds, once they cool down, an extremely important part of the ritual begins. Of course, temperature is very important in this process. Too high would reduce all the bones to ashes and too low would not reduce the rest of the body to ashes.

The family enters the chamber and proceeds to collect the bones of the deceased. This is done within an order and ceremony. Starting with the foot bones, and using wooden sticks, the bones are deposited one by one in an urn, along with the ashes, following the order that the bones have in the skeleton. This task would be carried out by a man and a woman. This practice of including the energies of the feminine and masculine alike, I have already observed in indigenous rituals in North America, so I assume that it is part of that animist heritage of the Kotsuage. We can only assume that this is done in an attempt to preserve the remains in a harmonious way, as close as possible to their original order. Although there is a bone that is reserved for the end, the thymus, which due to its particular appearance, looks like a Buddha in a lotus position and its spiritual properties. This bone would be the bridge between the head and the body, the brain and the heart. The thymus would be the last bone to enter the urn and seal the remains.

All members would partake of this collection of bones, as part of the honours rendered to the deceased. Once saved, the remains would be honoured by the family for a minimum of 49 days after which the remains would be buried, although the Japanese government implemented new legislation on Natural Funerals, where families can scatter the ashes outside of a tradition or traditional cemeteries.

After the Kotsuage, the remains of the deceased would remain in the custody of the family until they were scattered or buried. According to custom, only after the deceased are honoured on a certain number of occasions, they become part of the family ancestors; from when the person dies until more or less 100 years pass, with intermittent ceremonies to honour his memory. 7 years after his death, at 13, 23, 27, 33, 49 and 100 years, consecutively.

From my western point of view but as a practitioner of animist rites, I find Kotsuage a wonderful practice. Not only because it allows you to be in direct contact with the bones of your ancestors during the ritual, but also because it also gives you the possibility of keeping some of the bones, if you decide not to bury them all. As relics these bones can be passed among the family and honoured in a common altar to the ancestors. What an amazing possibility.

Imelda, a Norse Witch

Imelda Almqvist is a shamaness and witch from the northern lands of Europe. She is a bone collector who explores the northern woods. It is curious that she, like myself, although in different latitudes, has also heard the call of the Bone Mother, a deity whose origin is lost in time, at the dawn of spirituality in Europe.

But this is not by chance, the Bone Mother is present in Iberia too. Of course, she would have travelled from South to North with the melting of the glaciers that covered northern Europe. I personally feel that in some way the Bone Mother would be an ancient form of Goddess Cailleach in Iberia, in fact I represent the Goddess with a necklace made of bones, also bones hanging from her staff.

Imelda says about the Bone Mother:

> *As a daughter of The Bone Mother I am a Norse witch who gathers plants and cooks up medicines on the edge of the forest. A liminal figure. Her Cave is the Womb-Tomb and Dream Incubation chamber where all life forms return at their journey's end. The Bone Mother lifts the mantle of false burdens, injurious projections and emotional pain. She invites us to make a fearless inventory of unlived dreams.*

Aaron, Hoodoo and Bones

Aaron is a Reverend, Rootworker, Santero and Espiritismo practitioner and has been exploring Lucumi-derived traditions for years. Aaron incorporates the use of bones into his practices and although it is a personal choice, he strongly recommends that this type of work be done under the supervision of a mentor and within a community that can provide support and that can provide adequate education on bone work.

I think it is important for the reader to understand the context of the use of bones within hoodoo, for this reason allow me to give you a quick overview about hoodoo before we continue exploring Aaron's practice. We find the roots of hoodoo in the African Diaspora and in the time of slavery in the United States, as an evolution of the different traditions of the slaves brought from Africa. Within this evolution we find that in certain places, the slaves also incorporate into their practices some customs and part of the folklore of the local natives.

Hoodoo is not a unique practice linked to a certain place in North America, since in reality it belongs to the entire black community. It doesn't matter where they are. Although there may be variations or differences in a practice at the individual level or even from one group or region to another, it is a common heritage within the community. Of course, they have gained fame for their local practices, or because their practitioners have achieved a certain popularity.

Within North American geography, we can perhaps highlight the practices in the Gulf of Mexico area and within Louisiana and the famous city of New Orleans. During the Haitian Revolution, a considerable number of mulattoes (term that was used back on those days to designate people of mixed white and black ancestry) ended up in this area of the United States, escaping the massacre of whites and mulattoes by the leaders of the slaves.

It should be noted that the inhabitants of Haiti had preserved in a purer way the traditions that came from West Africa with their ancestors. The reason for this would have been the Frenchified philosophy of the plantation owners in Haiti. Not only did they not separate the groups of slaves or families, but they tolerated the slaves celebrating their customs and speaking their own language. This did not happen on the mainland.

With the arrival at the end of 1700, to the shores of the Gulf, of that wave of refugees from Haiti, their practices also arrived. These practices rooted more deeply in Africa in many cases had been lost among the slaves of the continent. New Orleans, and its famous Congo Square, would become a kind of cultural centre and connection with the African Traditions that had been preserved in Haiti.

We can say that a cultural revolution took place in which these practices were integrated by the locals and went hand in hand with other religious practices such as the Christian ones and those of the Natives. From the amalgamation of traditions that occurred because of the African Diaspora, new traditions were born, like voodoo, spiritualism and obeah.

As happens in other places, we find that magic, in this case hoodoo, is used by slaves as a tool for survival. Hoodoo would not only have been used to save the lives of some slaves, but also, among other things, to soften the heart of the Master or even magically support the escape of a slave, as a kind of protection.

You may have heard of the famous voodoo Queen Marie Laveau (1794–1881). Today thousands of tourists visit her grave and related sites in the French Quarter. Equally famous was her teacher, known as Dr. John, also known as Bayou John. From his native Senegal he was taken to Cuba as a slave. Once he moved to New Orleans, he joined the voodoo community and became a very popular healer as well as a fortune teller.

Aaron shares with me that within hoodoo there are two main uses for bones:

The Use of Bones as a Method of Divination

Talking about the divination practice with bones, Aaron bases his practice on what he knows to be inherited from the old school. According to him, at the beginning people would have used chicken or opossum bones. In that old school, bones would have been thrown directly on the ground. The slavers would have assumed very likely that the enslaved people were simply gambling, which would have helped them to exercise this practice without being censored. Bones would not have been limited to being for private use, but would also have had great importance as a tool for the community. For example, the bones would have been consulted about a decision that directly affected the community, to find out the possible outcome.

Just like in practice with the shoulder blades of the Highlands, the meat of the animal would have been eaten and after having cleared the bones, the reading would have been carried out using each bone of the animal's skeleton, that is, the complete skeletons were used for the reading and each bone would have represented certain things for the practitioner. A bone would have represented abundance, another curses, another sexual desire and thus a meaning for each bone of the skeleton. Bones are used when the practitioner sees the need to delve deeper into a problem. Of course, the correspondences or variations in the interpretation would have varied from practitioner to practitioner, due to the fact that the hoodoo practice is not uniform and there are many variations in the practices.

Over time, the practice of reading the bones would evolve and incorporate other elements. Objects such as domino pieces, dice, nutmeg seeds, stones, arrowheads and others that have added symbolic amplitude to the reading. Today we find bone readers who, for example, combine hoodoo with styles, such as Sangoma, of which we find its origin in the practices of local shamans and healers in South Africa. Within this evolution, the bones are still there and despite the fact that there are new elements, we can say that the bones are still important.

Bones speak in many ways. Every detail of how they fall is important and whether they fall on one side or the other can change the meaning of the reading. Today there are people who incorporate mats with different designs to the reading of bones. The mat can help add depth or dimension to the reading, depending on where they fall within the particular design of each mat. But the truth is that it is also somehow facilitating the interpretive work. A move away from the origins and from the element of the ground — which perhaps added to the energy of reading. We would be limiting our own intuition by having so many tools.

Aaron emphasises that if you're a professional bone reader, it's very important to clean your bone set between clients, because if you don't, especially with a tool so connected to ancient work, we can give totally confused messages to the wrong person — and that is not acceptable or professional. He highly recommended one book by a particular author: Michel Jackson. *Bones, Shells, and Curios: A Contemporary Method of Casting the Bones*.

The Use of Bones as a Magical Ingredient for Mojos and Spells

Regarding the use of bones as a magical ingredient, we find that they are a common ingredient in different mojos or spells. It should also be noted that not only animal bones are used and that human bones are still a popular ingredient today. Linked to this popularity, we also find that tombs are looted, in search of the precious bones for spellcasting.

Teeth, dead man's fingers, hands, human skulls, crab claws, legs and skulls of different animals — the list of ingredients related to bones used to conjure is diverse and each of these ingredients has its own unique properties and they can be used for different purposes. We explore some of them in the magical/practical section of the book.

Bones within the Inuit Traditions

If we wanted to explore today how the ancestors' used bones, perhaps the closest way to do so would be to approach the Inuit traditions of the arctic.

Numerous archaeological excavations and studies carried out in the area conclude that since the first humans settled in the Arctic Circle, estimated about 5000 years ago, the people of the Arctic used bones not only to create artefacts of daily use but also over time, they used them as means of artistic expression. Even today, Inuit bone art is highly valued, it is not something that remains in the past.

But nowadays their art is far from what it was in the Paleo Inuit period or the Thule Inuit period. The tools created by this first group included harpoons, knives, scraping tools, made of walrus ivory, although remains made with non-marine animals, such as caribou antlers, have also been found. The Thule Inuit made larger and more varied bone tools that included buttons, sewing needles, combs, but the fact that they were everyday objects does not mean that they were not elaborate, since some of them had very elaborate carvings. Of course, the Inuit also made small sculptures, especially of polar animals like bears, walruses, birds, seals, whales... sometimes also anthropomorphic figures, although these are the least common ones.

Over time, the descendants of these first Inuit would trade these objects with European sailors who, within their fascination for Inuit art, would begin to make their version of these engravings. But not only the art of the Inuit began to change when it came into contact with the Europeans. Later, the Canadian government would promote the industrialization of tribal art, supposedly so that the natives would have their own source of income, but that it would also somehow influence the art of the natives. Although in the early 2000s a group was created to somehow safeguard and promote the typical art of the Inuit. Although this would not be the only political movement of the people of the Arctic Circle.

In the 1990s, the Inuit people began to raise their voices to protest about the remains of some of their ancestors being exhibited in museums and study of the remains of their ancestors and their grave goods. These appropriations, which occurred during the different excavations, provided the different museums with study material that actually belongs to the heritage of the Inuit people. With the creation of laws for indigenous rights in both Canada and the US, the Inuit are beginning to be given a voice. Sometimes their protests succeed and they manage to get several remains returned to them to be reburied.

Bones, Ink and Skin

In 1985 unearthed in Tennessee, in an old Native American burial ground in Fernvale, was what is to date considered the world's oldest tattoo set. The bones, especially sharp, and the traces of ink on bones and shells, left no doubt that the bundle belonged to a tattoo artist from about 3,600 years ago. This discovery shouldn't be so shocking, as tattooing was a common practice among Native Americans and we can find several references from settlers about Natives and their tattoos. I remember the story of a white woman, Olive Oatman, her parents were new settlers looking to relocate and she was captured and later adopted by the natives. They gave her a tattoo on her chin, some chronicles say, as part of a rite.

But the Fernvale tattoo tool kit is not the only one that was found. The remains of another tattoo tool kit was unearthed in Papua New Guinea, belonging, according to experts, to the Lapita culture. It's believed that this Neolithic culture extended from Melanesia, to Polynesia and Micronesia. The 15-piece kit found at the Solomon Islands, was made up of different points made of obsidian crystal and, what at first was believed to be pieces to clean hide, was confirmed by a scientific team to be tattoo tools from about 3,000 years ago.

But the use of bones in tattoo work is not something that was left in the past. Today there are hand poke tattoo artists who incorporate bone needles into their work or make their tools entirely out of bones. While there are people that travel the world looking to get a traditional tattoo or trying to learn old ways, the reality is that there are very few places where ritualistic tattoo traditions are preserved. A few years ago, as a connoisseur of the magical power of tattoo and as a shamaness, I started working with my spirits to seek help and new shamanic tools to work in the tattoo field. The intention was to be able to make sacred and ritual tattoo work accessible to anyone, and I managed to do it. My Bones, Ink and Skin program became a unique way of working, open to every tattoo artist from any background. Because it does not belong to any established tradition, it is part of the Path of the Bones and my personal work with the spirits in the realms and so I began to share my shamanic knowledge with tattoo artists. Those interested in the spiritual part of tattooing, to provide a holistic and healing experience to anyone who wants a shamanic ritual tattoo. In addition to the training for tattooers, I also organise retreats where I bring together tattoo artists and seekers of a ritual tattoo, where I guide the entire ritual process for them.

PART II

Chapter 1

The Path of the Bones

The Path of the Bones belongs to all of us, is not something strange or foreign to us. As you might now realise, it is a universal path that any person can walk, in connection with their own bones and with their ancestors, with the spirits that surround them. Walking this path, you learn to connect with who you are from all angles. From the work with the ancestors, to personal work, healing and exploring one's soul. This path is about being able to go through each part of your being as something complete — it is this holistic approach that makes this path what it is.

An important part of the work on this Path of the Bones is to see. And yes, it takes time and practice, but I don't think that anything you can achieve easily is really that helpful. Without hard work it becomes less valued. I may not be the easiest teacher, I may demand more than others, but I can't give anything away, because then I'm not doing anyone any favours. That's why I put my effort into making sure that those who work with me can "see" and guide their steps. At the end of the day, the vision is going to be important for them, not for me. I have my own visions and they are a very special part of my life.

I am a liminal being. One of my family's gifts is the gift of vision. My grandmother was a visionary and I was lucky that she shared some of those visions with me. My Uncle Manolo also has a special gift for perceiving the invisible. My mother is a visionary, as am I. As a Walker in Between the Worlds, I have been navigating multiple realities since I was very little, so I don't need a trance to get a vision. Of course, during trance work or when I use visionary plants, the visions are on another level, but many times these visions arrive without warning in my day-by-day life, and I make spontaneous journeys between different realities — crossing time and space. Sometimes I cross the dream portal as the threshold to other dimensions. I would like to share some of those visions with you that are related to bones.

La Huesera: Children of the Bone Mother

The Path of the Bones somehow opened up to me after going through a very difficult experience; fighting a lymphoma that I had in my heart. My lymphoma changed everything. I could no longer participate in the ceremonies and share with the group as I used to, due to my weakened heart. I fell into an abyss because of my illness, finding myself alone, excluded from my spiritual tribe.

It was there where La Huesera found me. Without strength, exhausted, poisoned, still spitting chemotherapy, vomiting the shadows that the ayahuasca grandmother had shown me. Somehow, I died. And La Huesera sang to me, she sang to my bones, tired of hospitals. My body floated in the air and the flesh began to leave my bones. Little by little, I saw my flesh dissolve into the shadows and only my skeleton remained. No organs, no flesh, no skin, nothing.

I don't know how long I was there, suspended in the air. The next thing I remember is seeing myself standing up, naked, but no longer a skeleton. "*Sing*" I heard. And I began to sing and then I remembered that my voice was part of my medicine and La Huesera asked me to sing louder and so I did and the drum of my heart began to play louder too. *"Follow me, follow me, she said, "follow your bones. Who lives in your bones?"* She asked. And I saw the face of my great-grandmother, my grandparents, the face of my parents and other faces that I did not know. I heard, *"I do, I live in your bones, I, and I..."* And I rode on the steppe in Central Asia and sailed seas, warmer, then colder, in different boats, different latitudes; I ran through the woods, and walked through the sand of the desert and through the ice of the Arctic, I witnessed wars, I felt thirsty, hungry; My bones ached, there was pain in my bones. Then blood and the waters of life ran down my legs, until they touched the ground, for each of the births that preceded me. I heard La Huesera say: *"Look out for them, look out for them in your own bones, this is the way... Sing to your bones, to the bones of others, take them with their ancestors, now you are part of me, sing Huesera."*

Who is La Huesera? The Bone Mother, The Bone Woman? It's been quite a few years since she came to me that vision and opened the Path of Bones for me. The funny thing is that now I am also a Huesera, but of course! I'm her daughter, we all are in a way Children of the Bone Mother.

At this point in my life, I feel that La Huesera (her name in Spanish), the Bone Mother, is perhaps the oldest Goddess that was ever worshipped. To me she is that primal goddess that emanated at the dawn of human spirituality. She who is a mother, a life giver but she is also death, keeper of our bones, guardian of the entrance to the primal otherworld as our ancestors knew it. And no, I am not inventing a new goddess here, she is as old as the first spiritual manifestations in relation to the dead, we are all connected to her and we can find her in different geographies around the planet. She is the Bird Goddess of the Vinca culture that Marija Gimbutas talked about. She is a shapeshifting goddess, perhaps she has come to you in another form, like a Bear Goddess or a Serpent Goddess. Our ancestors worshipped her and offered her their dead ones for her to guide them and help them cross over to the other side. Even before they gave her a name, she was already a powerful deity, so powerful that she has survived to this day, only you may not be aware that you know her, even if it is by another name. Because she has many names. For me she is the most powerful goddess of the northern hemisphere and yet, she has been hiding under many guises. The Bone Mother as I feel her, came from the East and conquered the whole of Europe.

The Bone Mother is very much alive and is also very relevant to many people under her different aspects and names. Connecting with her is not difficult, as I said, somehow, we are all her children, she lives in the memory of each one of the ancestors that we carry in us, she lives in our bones. She is the eternal old woman, the giant hag who walks among the stone circles and standing stones across Europe and roams in the caverns that gave refuge to our ancestors. You might not be aware of her presence, but she is here, I have felt her especially strong in my land, in Iberia, quite possibly due to the importance of the Iberian Peninsula as a bridge between Africa and Europe, also as a refuge for the first humans while Northern Europe was under the ice. Caves are very suitable places to connect with her. There are many caves in Iberia, some well-known, others not so much. Where I lived in Granada, the Valle de Lecrin, there are many caves. The Valley is a special place that held human settlements from the Upper Palaeolithic. The place was idyllic to settle in, because of its special geography, the many shelters and lots of water, at the foot of the Sierra Nevada. We find in those caves and chasms, the remains of those first humans who lived there all those years ago and The Bone Mother guarded them. She did so through those first ages, to the Age of Metals. The Valle de Lecrin is rich in metal deposits and saw many people prosper in the territory over the centuries. From those first people to the first Iberian settlements to be followed by the Mediterranean traders and later the first Roman to follow till our present day.

It is no coincidence that the land of my ancestors, in the West of Granada, has an important history of settlements throughout the times. The region of Entre Rios is not only rich in water, it is also one of the few places that still have its original forest, which has been preserved among its mountains over the millennia, with a great abundance of wild animals. The northern slopes of the Sierra de Almijara and Tejeda are not only a natural and geological wonder, with a large number of caves and the particularity of its soil, its fauna and flora are also amazing, with various endemic species inhabiting the mountains. It is also an archaeological paradise that is yet to be fully explored. Unfortunately, being such an isolated place, it is usually left out of state investments, a terrible reality since we find in the region important necropolis, dolmens and remains of different civilizations. But of course, being a hidden gem also helps to preserve its beauty. These are the lands of the Bone Mother in Southern Europe and I have had the privilege of growing up there, as a wild child in those mountains and the Bone Mother held my wee hand.

Of course, I also felt the Bone Mother strong in Eastern Europe, you can breathe her there deep in the forest. I even felt her in Norway, even North of Morocco during my many travels. Now that I live in Scotland, I go to her encounter to certain places that the legends say she has created, as The Cailleach but in reality, she is with me wherever I go. Because I am her Priestess and I walk her Path of The Bones.

A Sea of Bones: Meeting the Skeleton Woman

Allow me to share with you a vision that haunted me for days, as if part of me had never really returned from that realm. I'm sure I need to go back and finish something, but for now let me tell you how I came to meet the Skeleton Woman.

It is no coincidence that on the three occasions that I have gone to the beach this summer I have found bones, as if each meeting had been like a prelude or a key to prepare my encounter with Skeleton Woman. The first occasion was the complete skeleton of a sheep, in Dunure. Right on the beach, on the edge of the pastures. I was tempted to collect the bones but it still smelled too rotten and I had my two little kids with me, but there it was. Of course, I would have loved to have taken the skull! On the second occasion, I was playing with my children in the pools created by the low tide in North Ayrshire. There were a couple of seagulls nearby and I tried not to let the children get too close or leave them alone. I remember speaking to the seagulls in my head and asking them where I could find one of their bones for a spell that you will find in this book. As if by magic, five minutes after asking my question, there in front of me, inside the pool of water, I saw a bone, half buried in the sand. I took it with ceremony and thanked the seagulls for their gift. On the third occasion, we were walking along a quiet beach on the Isle of Arran. As I always do, I was looking for treasures in the sand and to my surprise, next to some shells I found a small and sharp bone, it was broken to create the point. I put the bone in my bag and we went home. The next morning, at dawn, right in the stage that you are between sleep and wakefulness, there I met her.

Clarissa Pinkola Estes describes her in one of her stories from her famous book *Women Who Run with Wolves*:

She had done something of which her father disapproved, although no one any longer remembered what it was. But her father had dragged her to the cliffs and thrown her over and into the sea. There, the fish ate her flesh away and plucked out her eyes. As she lay under the sea, her skeleton turned over and over in the currents.

The truth is that I had completely forgotten about the Skeleton Woman, the protagonist of a popular story of the Inuit people. It had been so many years since I re-read her book that I didn't remember her. It is no coincidence that I feel very connected to Sedna. Also, I found out some years ago that I had Inuit ancestors from Greenland.

I found myself walking along the beach, with some bones in my hand. I found my diving goggles on the shore. I took them and put them on and headed to the water. I was walking on the seabed, and I noticed how something was approaching me from behind. When I turned around, she was there, right in front of me. All bones, some rags of old clothes still hanging from her, her empty eye sockets staring into my eyes, black hair, decorated with some seaweed, floating in the water. My glasses disappeared and my clothes disappeared and I found myself naked, in front of her, both of us suspended in the water, like a reflection of mortality and vitality of the same energy. At times I didn't know where she ended and I began. Her bones were my bones, my flesh, her flesh, all thoughts vanished from my mind. It was just her and me, underwater. The next thing I remember was seeing myself on the shore again, with some seaweed in my hair, my face changing from a skeleton to me, from me to a skeleton … And that's how my vision ended.

Pick a Bone

This is a vision that until now I have not shared with anyone. Somehow, I think it was this vision that led me to think that the bones The Cailleach was keeping were human, because at the time I thought it was her I had met in my vision.

I found myself walking down a dirt road at sunset and it was cold. Not far away there was a trail of smoke rising from a chimney. Approaching the cottage, I saw a light inside and ventured to knock on the door.

A very old woman who reminded me a little of my great-grandmother opened the door, but this woman was very tall. Although I assumed that she had shrunken with age, she was still much taller than me, at least three heads. Although her face was lined with wrinkles, she had a curious gleam in her eyes.

I told her honestly that I didn't know what I was doing there, to which she replied with a friendly tone that she did and invited me to sit down. I realised that I had spent so much time looking at her that I had barely looked around. It was a peculiar cottage, everything seemed bigger than normal. The table, the chairs, even the fireplace was huge, and inside the fireplace a cauldron was set aside from the fire. I actually felt small, given the size of everything I saw. It became clear to me that this was indeed the home of a giant. While I was sitting in a rocking chair, she took a bucket from the kitchen and said, *I'll be right back*.

I don't know how long she was absent, because I stayed absorbed looking at the fire, feeling relaxed despite being in a strange house. I felt at peace, knowing that I was safe. Returning she left the bucket next to her chair and took a large bowl from the kitchen which she placed in front of my feet. Then she opened the lid of the cauldron and with a large ladle, filled the bowl. Back in the kitchen she returned with a cup of tea that smelled of licorice. I looked at the bowl and it seemed like a type of broth, one of those recipes that takes a long time to make. She nodded as if she agreed with me, as if she had read my thoughts. I approached the bucket. When looking inside

I was unsurprised to see bones, bones that seemed human. I nodded again and she told me in a solemn way: *They are your bones.* That statement left me a little baffled. How could they be my bones? To which she continued speaking. *I know you're lost, at least right now. I thought that maybe I could help you, bringing some of your ancestors.* And she was right, of course.

She explained to me that each of those bones belonged to an ancestor. In the bucket there were bigger bones and smaller ones. I was curious. Then she took my hand and with a small sharp knife cut the tip of one of my fingers on my left hand. The blood began to flow, falling into the bowl. My blood mixed with the broth, forming spirals and drawings. The old giantess lady then started to perform a kind of prayer, almost whispering. Then she instructed me to take a deep breath, close my eyes and pick a bone from the bucket. And so, I did in a ceremonious way, asking my ancestors for support. After I picked the bone, she told me to throw it in the bowl.

What happened next was totally unexpected. As the bone touched the bowl, the broth began to steam and emit a strange light. I looked carefully and began to see images and a face formed in the broth and after that, a figure emerged from the bowl, standing in front of us. I then proceeded to introduce myself to the spirit as blood of her blood and bone of her bone, to which she responded by nodding. The old woman spoke to me mentally and she instructed me to ask the spirit how she could help me, which I did.

The spirit of my ancestor began to speak and I listened carefully. Whenever I meet my ancestors it's special; but this time it wasn't about them. It wasn't about understanding their stories, like when I visit them in the Cave of Souls. So, I listened, for a long time, to everything my ancestor had to tell me — and I cried a river. I asked what my options were and the best way to go, trying to understand. My ancestor replied without omitting details, which I appreciated. Out of curiosity I asked how her story was related to mine and she briefly summarised her experience in this plane of existence and I understood why I had taken her bone and not another.

The old lady asked me if I was sure I didn't want to ask her anything else, and after thinking about it for a moment I asked her several more questions. After I got my answers, I asked my ancestor what she preferred as an offering, to thank her for her help and I made a mental note of what she asked me to do for her. I thanked her again and we proceeded to close the ritual. Following the instructions of the old woman, I took the bone from the broth while she recited some words and between steam and spectral light the spirit of my ancestor disappeared.

I sat back in the rocking chair to meditate on everything I had heard and thanked the giant old woman for her help. I asked her how she had bones from my ancestors and she replied that she kept many bones, to which I simply nodded. She handed me a cloth with which to dry my ancestor's bone and returned it to her. When I asked if I could come back to work with the rest of the bones, she agreed and she also told me that I could stay for the night. The wind was roaring outside and there was no moon. It was a dark and cold November night and the old woman's house was cosy. She got up and took the bucket of bones disappearing through a door. When she came back, I was almost asleep in the rocking chair and she asked me to follow her. When she opened the big cabinet on one side of the room, it was no cabinet, it was actually a lovely big bed. She invited me to fall asleep, which I did quickly. It felt like a wool mattress, like the ones my grandmother used to have years ago. I remember the closet door closing and her words: *Tomorrow will be another day*.

The Dead King

In this journey-dream I found myself lost in the fog. But it wasn't all fog, despite the morning mist, there was smoke, from unextinguished fires and if my nose wasn't deceiving me, it also smelled like pitch, I even thought I could smell blood. Sometimes I don't know if my sense of smell is a curse or a blessing. On this occasion it was undoubtedly telling me that there had been a battle and I was sure that when I started prowling through the fog and smoke, I was going to find myself in quite a dramatic situation. I hadn't taken a step when I ran into the first corpse and this was followed by more and next to them spears, swords, shields and mutilated horses.

I walked for a while between corpses, I couldn't help but pray for them, not wanting to look too closely, but it was very difficult not to see. The morning fog dissipated and the fire in the nearby fields died down when there was nothing left to be burned. Fire clings to wood when it burns, but grain burns like paper. I saw some come to pick up people, perhaps those injured and they began to erect funeral pyres for some of their dead on the spot. Of course, in that chaos I didn't dare to talk to anyone. It's funny but when I travel it's like there's a filter that allows me to understand any language. Sometimes I'm glad I almost always wear a black poncho covering my clothes, they possibly thought I was a woman looking for her dead ones.

I saw someone who appeared to be a priest. I think they were looking for high-ranking soldiers, maybe some prince and I saw how they carried a corpse to a funeral pyre with a lot of ceremony. A carriage pulled by two horses arrived and two women got out of it. An older woman and a younger one, with a child still hanging from her breast. What I saw was hard to watch, but I understood that it was part of a ritual. The older woman, I assumed that she was the mother of the deceased, approached the corpse with a knife and nailed it to the chest of her deceased son, removing the heart from his chest. The priest approached with a box and they put it there. Then with her hands still stained with her son's blood, she approached the widow with the baby, who sobbed inconsolably, and to my surprise she marked her and the baby's face with the blood of her dead son while she murmured some words that I did not get to hear.

A black ram was brought forward and the Priest proceeded to sacrifice it. Libations were made, and he began what was clearly a necromantic ritual, to speak with the deceased. At this point I got closer, as there were very few witnessing this scene. Possibly only some other people of importance in the court, the priest, the queen mother and the widow. Various gods were invoked, I assumed local underworld deities. The Queen Mother took an active part, which led me to think that she might have been a priestess at some point or an initiated of the mysteries. She danced pleadingly, begging her son to help them foresee the future of his kingdom. The Priest entered a trance and announced that the king was willing to answer their questions. The Queen Mother then asked: *Who should rule the kingdom until your son, the prince becomes an adult?* After a moment of silence, the priest-king said: *His mother.* The Queen Mother then asked another question: *The Queen Regent. What should they do with her?* The priest replied that the Queen Regent had to remarry, but he did not give any names on this occasion. The Queen Mother then asked: *What will the future bring for the little prince?* to which the priest replied that everything depended on who the Queen married. He said that a bad marriage could bring the death of the prince and that they had to find her husband away from the throne, far from those who now wanted to sit on it. Her new husband would come from far away, beyond the borders of the city, beyond the seas. The Queen's new husband would be a foreigner. He continued that he would not be interested in being King of this land, because he was already King of his own, but he would be the father of new kings. The young Queen would be the mother of four kingdoms, each of them with one of her children on the throne and among her children there would also be a princess. This girl would have to be educated on mysteries. The last words were for the Queen Mother, he commissioned his mother to take care of his wife and son and after saying this, the spirit of the dead King left the body of the priest and he came out of the trance. The Queen Mother looked at the young Queen with a strange expression but went over to her and took her by the hand. Together they got into the chariot and left, taking with them the King's heart.

The priest and his assistants lift the King's body to the pyre where he was to be cremated. Later his bones were deposited in an urn and taken to the royal mausoleum.

As if it were a movie, I saw time speed up, I saw the Queen Mother making preparations behind the council. The end of the mourning came and the conflicts between some of the advisers of the council began. Of course, the Queen Mother had loyal people by her side. When she had everything ready, one night, secretly, a small caravan left the palace. The travellers included the Queen Mother, the young Queen, the Prince, plus their elite soldiers and servants. They would leave the city to undertake a long journey, taking a false identity where they would pass themselves off as a widowed princess and her mother. Meanwhile in the palace, that same night, the councillors who were trying to take over the kingdom were assassinated by order of the Queen Mother. Everything was chaos for a few days, but the Prince and the women were already far away, away from danger and nobody, not even the Priest, knew which route they had taken. The leaders of the army, loyal to the Queen Mother, quickly restored order and the kingdom-city awaited the return of the Queens and the Prince. They travelled far, far across the sea and had dozens of adventures, but then my time to return to this reality had come, and the visions of the two women dissolved as I came back.

Following the Footsteps of Your Ancestors

The Path of the Bones is a place of reconnection, healing and empowerment. Because of the importance of diving into the nature of our bones, into the history of who we are. Because the reality is that we do not know who we really are, and that leaves us in a very fragile position in this society. Because instead of building our identity from within, unfortunately, it is now being built from the outside, with accessory qualities, alien to us. Lacking the strength of blood, of family identity, an identity that in the past we even saw in our surnames, in the suffix son, in what indicated that we were children of ... for example, Jorgenson, Orson, Grayson, Jackson, Jameson.

Ok, there may be family stories that are not ideal to pass on from parents to children, all families have skeletons in their closets, but we have stopped talking about our ancestors. The reality is that today, we have stopped passing on family stories, those stories that were shared by the fire or at the table. Now we are lucky if we can eat at the table without someone connected to their phone.

This is a path of consciousness. Not only does it give us the opportunity to connect with our ancestors, but also to rebuild a forgotten or unknown identity. Because this work is so powerful that I myself have witnessed how even people who had been adopted managed to meet their blood family and hear their story from their lips. I have seen such people find healing and understanding, peace, after a lifetime of internal struggle. I even remember the encounter between the two mothers, the adoptive mother and the natural mother in the shamanic worlds. Such is the scope of the ancestral work as I understand it and my work on the Path of the Bones.

While family or systemic constellations depend on the interpretation of the guide or therapist, I make sure that the person seeking help on the Path of the Bones actively participates, for several reasons. The first because I firmly believe that the person consulting has to be the recipient of the power of the experience and this is achieved by standing aside as a shaman and holding the consultation. Allowing and guiding the person so that they can safely navigate the shamanic worlds to find that power that is hidden in each process. The second reason is that living the experience as an active subject cannot be compared to being only the recipient of information channelled for you.

But to be able to work in this way, you have to be willing to go beyond what is established and break the rules of what is understood as good practice. By breaking the rules, sometimes I have found people so stuck in the old ways that it has been impossible for me to work with them, even if I wanted to help them. Because they were not able to get out of the box where they had put the shamanic practices. If I have learned anything from working with spirits and outside the box it is that there is no box and that there is no limit to what we can do in our work between realities if we truly surrender to the spirits.

And in ancestral work we have to be especially open to knowing. It doesn't matter what information we find, because every drop of that information is you. They are part of your traumas, your fears, it is your strength and your tastes (which can also be inherited). Because we carry much more weight than you think from our ancestors when it comes to who you are. Only we are not aware of it. Up to this point we have been exploring the bones outwards, now it is time to explore the bones inwards.

Beyond the Bones

Beyond the bones, beyond the connection with the ancestors, of course, the work on the Path of the Bones is not limited to ancestral work. It is, as I have already expressed, a holistic path since we are highly complex beings. Our reality is a cocktail of the weight of our blood and bones but also of the soul load that we bring to this incarnation. That karmic load is responsible for many of our experiences in this life. As part of this path, we also explore our soul history, we cross space-time to understand that burden and its repercussions on this plane of existence. When it comes to healing the soul, not everything is related to the past, so it is also important to revisit and work to heal the cracks or loss of soul that occurred in this incarnation.

But perhaps the work that I enjoy sharing the most from the Path of the Bones is teaching people how to shapeshift. The technique never ceases to amaze students or the people who come to an experimental day. Because in the past, the shapeshifting technique was reserved for only a few shamans, who were capable of transforming. Shapeshifting has incredible healing potential, not only because of the healing that we can obtain during the process, by becoming an animal we somehow channel its strength and it is a super empowering experience. Although it seems incredible, I started this work to help women who were in their last stage of pregnancy, to connect them with the animal side in preparation for childbirth. Of course, then I saw that it could benefit others aside from pregnant women, so I began to share the technique with everyone. Specially to help people who were very weak when they came to me. Animal spirits are extremely generous, over time their help went beyond the simple transformation of the person and became a true blessing.

I had never stopped to notice how many different journeys had opened up for me in the shamanic worlds until someone asked me to please do a training based only on healing journeys. At that time, I counted 18 different journeys, right now I think there are already 20, maybe more. The work in the shamanic worlds cannot be pigeonholed, the worlds are mutable and when I have needed something different for someone, the worlds have opened a new door, a new place to find answers and healing. Nor can you enter aimlessly, because you only lose energy and efficiency in your work. This is what happens when there is a total surrender to the world of spirits and the invisible. Now my students open new doors themselves, with the help of their spirits and the work that I transmit to them changes with them and expands according to their needs.

But not everything is working in other realities, also the physical work that we do on this plane can be very powerful. Lucky me, apart from my incredible spirit guides, I also had the honour of learning with incredible teachers. From them, I have learned to work on the soul of the person with an almost surgical precision. Because if it is important to know the shamanic worlds and the possibilities of healing in that reality, it is almost as important to know the human soul at a physical level, to know how to identify the different layers of the soul and to be able to find objects or entities alien to the soul of the person, wounds, soul cracks or holes, blockages etc. Over the years the soul diagnosis I learned evolved with my personal practice. This type of diagnosis, or energetic reading of the soul, is a super tool. We no longer depend on going and journeying aimlessly to see what we find wrong with a person, the diagnosis has an amazing precision when it comes to finding something that is wrong, parasites, etc. That makes it much easier to be able to design a personalised action plan using shamanic techniques to assist the person.

So, sure, there's a lot more than just bones on this path. A very important part of it is to find personal tools. The final aim in this path will be to become the only tool that we are going to need to be able to carry out a shamanic healing session. No drum, no rattles, no crystals, no accessories, just you and the energy and spirits that you can move, to carry out your healing work.

Chapter 2

Bone Casting and Magic

Sourcing Bones for Your Practice

For our magical work we are going to need bones. Of course, today we can get bones in many ways, but perhaps it is somewhat more difficult now to get bones than it was 50 or 100 years ago. Especially for urbanites. Yes, there are specialised websites and etsy is also a good place to look for bones, but perhaps these purchased bones lack the energy of the moment when you find a bone in nature or the energy preparing and cleaning the bones of the animals you consume if you are a carnivore.

If we choose to buy bones, there's nothing wrong with that, but it is good to take some time before using them magically. We know it came from that store, but we don't know how they got there or the story behind it. It is always good to try to connect with them, purify them on an energetic level and of course, as a shaman, I strongly recommend doing a shamanic journey to speak with the spirit of the animal. Apart from being able to pay our respects in person, we can find out if the animal requires us to do something for them before we start using them, maybe they want a special offering. It doesn't matter that you bought the bone. Apart from the connection that you can create with the bone in this plane, imagine how beautiful it is to be able to create a connection in the spirit world with it. It's such a gift to be able to connect with any bones in this way. But before we learn how to do that journey, let's see where we can find bones.

Bones in Nature

The truth is that finding bones is sometimes a matter of luck. It is easier to find bones in nature, especially in the mountains.

I found my first big bone in the Sierra de Cazorla and it was a 5-pointed deer antler. When I was younger, the school took us to see the skeleton of a whale that had been stranded in the port, but I was too small to appreciate it. The deer antler was my first big forest trophy. As I lived in the mountains by the coast, I also saw many skeletons of little animals, I saw how the ants cleaned the corpses.

When you find fresh corpses either you take them to clean them before they start to rot or you can leave them somewhere to decompose naturally. This is usually a good idea with birds if you're not very good with a knife. I remember once I found a raven on the road many years ago, I made a deal with the raven and took it to a nicer place. I placed it by the roots of an oak tree and when pulling its tail, I got three feathers. You can cover the animal with leaves if it's too big and if small you could directly bury it. The little animals on the ground will do their job and if you give it some time and mark the place well, you can return to get a clean set of bones. Of course, small animals will not need too much time, while a larger animal will need more.

There are animals that, if in a hot country, will dry out in the sun or because of the high temperatures if they die, such as small reptiles or frogs, as well as insects like beetles. It would not be the first time that I have found a dry salamander behind a terracotta vase on the terrace. I remember that more than once, I have left a small dead bug or animal next to an anthill as an offering. Sometimes you find little birds that have fallen from the nest under the trees, the ants tend to get to them fast, at least in the south of Spain. I have to admit I haven't seen many ants where I live now, in Scotland.

With larger animals it is more difficult. If you are lucky and you find yourself with a complete skeleton, it is ideal, but you may find an animal that has recently died and that you cannot transport by yourself. Either you seek help or you can always take a part of it to clean it at home. Whatever it is, bigger or smaller, I recommend leaving an offering and making a prayer for the spirit of the animal.

Although I am not a fan of sport hunting or trophy hunting, if you hunt to eat or feed your family, this can be done with honour and I do not see anything dirty in it. The fisherman fishes from the sea and the sea is a mother who provides you with food. If you live in the mountains, she is your mother and you will not go short of food if you take care of her and respect her creatures and domain. Hunting for food is not disrespectful. It is disrespectful to hunt an animal to steal its head and hang it above your fireplace and let its meat rot in the mountains. I don't like guns, I think there is no fairness if you use a rifle, but bowhunting is another story. Most of the people I mix with now, go into the woods armed with a forager's knife at most.

It's funny how the bones we find in the mountains can disgust some people and yet the bones we find on the beach are romantic in a way. But let's face it, collecting shells on the beach is another story. In addition, the sea and the sand clean and polish them, like sea glass. I think we have all found shells by the sea and I personally cannot be on the beach without looking for treasures in the sand. Sometimes you not only find shells, you may also find some marine animals. I usually find a lot of crab remains and the claws are very useful in some spells. You may also find a dead fish or marine mammal on the beach. When this happens, it does make me sad but, we can always honour the animal in some way. We can also recycle old bone beads. I have bought old bone necklaces on ebay and recycled them to make something completely new.

Tips to Clean Bones

When you are ready to clean bones there are several ways to do it. I have already mentioned that they can be buried. You can also put them in water to boil. Anyone who has made a chicken soup like our grandmothers did, over three hours or more on the stove, knows that the meat comes off the bone and they usually come out of the soup quite clean. You can boil the bones for several hours but be careful because if they are too fine, they can soften and split. I have heard of people using baking soda sometimes in water. If you boil them, you can always brush them after, you can use a nail brush. Brushing can remove any bits left and you can spray the bones with alcohol afterwards.

There are people who, despite the fact that the bones may have some stains, leave them natural and do not whiten them. Other people, however, prefer to bleach the bones. You can carry out this process with household bleach, although if you leave the bones too long, they also soften. You can also use peroxide, like the one used by hairdressers or the laundry peroxide that is used to put in the washing machine for whitening clothes. I do not recommend leaving the bones in chemicals for more than 24 hours because sometimes the soft tissue of the bone can be damaged.

For the energetic cleansing part, you can use the same method that you use to cleanse any object that you are going to use with magical intentions, as you do in your usual practice or tradition. But that part is also very important, especially when the bones have not been found by us, if they came from a store or were given as a gift. You never know who has had them or how they have used them until the moment they reach your hands.

Bone Tools for Our Magical Work

Of course, beyond using the bones to display them in our magical space, we can use them for our rituals. Everything also depends on who you are going to work with at an energetic level or the intention of your work. Bone is also a very special material for making amulets or even bone figures, especially of ancient deities. Here in Scotland in 1860 Buddo, a 5,000-year-old carved whalebone idol, was unearthed from Skara Brae in Orkney and abundant bone-carved fetishes and tools from prehistoric times have been found. If our ancestors did it, why can't we? Plus, it's a way to connect with them too.

Animal skulls are very popular because in addition to being very striking, we can use them as a vessel and we can also use them for divination and necromantic practices. Of course, human skulls also, but personally, I do not want the skull of any stranger, without knowing where it has come from or if it has been stolen from a tomb. I really prefer to work with animal bones. We can use bone needles to embroider something special as an offering or create magical clothes, we can create a bone pen to write with ink, we can also create small totemic amulets, to work with the energy of an animal or create small amulets bottles with their bones. Bone knives are also very good, you can use them as an athame or for rituals that require a cutting object. We can use animal teeth to protect ourselves from the evil eye, from enemies, as well as claws. They used to be used as a charm for babies. Of course, full bird wings are another thing you can use, as well as loose feathers. Remember that shells are also bones!

What bones do we use? Depends. If it is for carving, I recommend cow bones, they are easier to work with, the thicker the better. If you know how to draw you can transfer your drawing to the bone and work the design with a Dremel type tool. You can even use pyrography, being careful. Of course, we can just use the bones, we don't need to manipulate them. In this sense, any bone would do, even if it is a fragment.

The work with the ancestors goes beyond a specific date, an anniversary. Several traditions directly relate the ancestors to winter or to the direction of the North on the medicine wheel, but for me the season of the ancestors begins earlier. The season begins for me with the winds of Autumn, in the last days of September. It is true that the vast majority of people who honour their deceased, tend to focus on celebrating at the end of October and the beginning of November. But our ancestors stay with us a few more days, after the celebrations of All Saints. About a week or ten days before the end of November comes the silence. At least that's how I perceive it. Remember that the calendar is a human invention, the months of the Gregorian calendar have suffered changes over time, and there are other calendars. Our ancestors were governed by the solstices and the equinoxes, by the seasons. It is difficult to give an exact date, I can only share an approximate date, how I feel it personally.

Working with the Ancestors

Our dead ones go silent and from that moment, there is only space for the silent song of winter; a tune of blizzards, cold and snow, depending on the latitude. The white of snow, like the white hair of the elders. It doesn't matter what tradition you follow, everyone can honour their ancestors. While for many, the death of a loved one is the end of a relationship, for me it is more of a transformation. In fact, I still feel very connected to several of my ancestors who are no longer in this reality. Especially my maternal Grandmother and Great-grandmother. They approach without warning; I notice their presence or they send me signals. Of course, I can go visit them in the shamanic worlds but it seems nice to feel them so close on this plane.

Establishing communication with the ancestors does not have to be complicated. We have discussed the power of blood. As carriers of their legacy of blood, we should not put limits on our approach to them. Also, it should be something to share with the family in a normalised way. Not something to be practised only in Latin American countries, but globally. Perhaps moving away from painful memories to get closer to a celebration of their lives and the good times we shared together. There are several cultures that celebrate their dead in a happy way, even at funerals.

As a Mediterranean woman I have been brought up within the cultural figure of the mourner. I never saw my Great-grandmother wear any colour other than black. My Grandmother began to mourn very young when her father died. In Spain, mourning went beyond simply dressing in black. Mourning restricted you socially too, especially if you were a woman. And it was even worse if you were young, since your social life ended while you mourned. You couldn't go to meetings, or festivals, or the movies, or parties in general. It was frowned upon if someone saw you chatting on the street, even worse if you were talking to a man. It was really restrictive. Some women couldn't even go outside without a black veil over their face, because while you were grieving, you had to somehow disappear. The men had it somewhat easier, for them mourning did not go beyond wearing a black bow on the hat or putting on some black buttons.

The status of the family member who passed away, determined how long one had to wear black. The periods of mourning used to be as follows: due to widowhood, two years and six months of mourning; for the loss of a child, another two years plus six months; for a father or mother, one year and six months; for grandparents or siblings, six months; for uncles or first cousins, three months.

It is worth noting that in rural areas, these periods were lengthened, for example, some widows wore black for life, like my Great-grandmother. Unfortunately, there were women who spent their lives dressed in black, due to the deaths of family members. Of course, it could be the case that a woman in mourning could marry, perhaps the date was already arranged before the death of the relative. The wedding would go ahead but even if a marriage did take place, the bride would have to be married in black.

After leaving the complete black dress code, they went on to wear half mourning, that is to say, you could combine black with other colours, although not of the happiest range, white, grey or mauve. I think my Grandmother had a camel-coloured jacket in the closet but I don't remember that she put it on and I think that after many years, I saw her with a navy-blue cardigan.

When you see people dressed in black because they're in mourning, it's like living in constant connection with death. Death is not something strange. Black is the memory that death is very close to us. It becomes familiar in a way, it's your loved ones who wear black, representing death.

Nowadays wearing mourning clothes has almost disappeared in many places. Young people are not willing to sacrifice their colours for black. Perhaps in rural areas there are people who still dress in black, although not for such long periods of time. The custom of wearing black is slowly dying. I see it in my mother's town, a place lost in the mountains in Granada. People born after the 1970's don't dress in black anymore, maybe for a few days but that's it. In reality, there was too much pain and coercion linked to mourning, so it is understandable that they want to leave the tradition behind.

We can honour our ancestors without having to sacrifice our style or way of life chained to a colour. A very easy way to honour them is to create an ancestor altar.

Building an Altar for Our Ancestors

While trying to establish a communication or relationship with the divine or invisible, for me the construction of an altar is very important. The altar is a way to focus the energies and to anchor the connection. Building an altar is a job that I take very seriously, precisely because I understand how sacred it is. It is a way of bringing the sacred to my space or to any space. The altar is a connector between worlds, between realities, it is a liminal place within your reality, something like a portal. When I travel and I have to hold sacred space, I usually start by clearing the space and building an altar, even if it's a modest one and will only be up for a few hours.

No matter where I go, near or far, I always start my work like this. I usually travel with some elements that, for me, are important for the work, for what they symbolise or their energy, and I put them on the altar. I also usually leave notes for attendees to bring things for the altar. When you place something on the altar, you are already making a clear sign to the spirits or deities that you are willing to work with them, that you are there to do the work. Your offering for the altar in this sense is a personal dedication and a way to honour the energies or divinities with whom we are working.

When we create an altar to the ancestors, for me it is always very special and also very personal. We are no longer building a connection with something foreign to us, this is an altar to our blood, to our bones. Although the function itself is the same, there is a palpable energetic difference when working with an ancestor altar. Of course, it is more earthy to begin with. Sometimes it also feels heavier and of course, an ancestor altar is a place where we are working with energies that are close to us. We are going to meet some of our ancestors, with whom we have shared an emotional bond. Though when we honour our ancestors, we are honouring all those who preceded us, even if we have a special union with those who have been part of our lives.

There are some basics to building an altar to our ancestors: photos, objects or jewels of the family heirloom. Fresh flowers are great, candles, fresh bread and fruits. We can even cook some food we know they used to like. Something I learned while working with ancestors is that those who lived in the interwar period shared a liking for chocolate and sweets as offerings. Perhaps because during those years they were a luxury that only a few could buy.

It really isn't complicated, no ritual is necessary to connect with them. While we are creating our altar, we are putting energy into it. And it can be as simple as spending time at the altar, saying a prayer for them, thanking them, remembering them. Even just sitting by the altar and sharing stories with our children about their ancestors. The best magic is found if it is done with love.

Of course, if you want to do ancestral shamanic work, you can do it in front of your altar or in the same room. When I share ancestral group work, we do so with our altar for the ancestors of the attendees in the centre of the room as the focal point and us sitting or lying around it. In addition to having your altar for them during the season of the ancestors, it is worth making shamanic journeys to visit weekly or every two weeks. I have a very special program to work with the ancestors between October and November, which I prepared for myself and which

I now also share with other people, to help them connect with their ancestors.

Shamanic Journey to Connect with the Land and the Ancestors

This is one of the Shamanic Journeys that I share on the Path of the Bones and we can actually go visit our ancestors in the world below, through the Cave of Souls and in other ways. This is a special journey because the intention is not only to try to establish a connection with the ancestors, but also with the land they walked on. This is quite a different journey since we are not going to the realm below. It is, so to speak, a journey in three levels. In addition, there is the component of space, time and the memory that is archived in the places. It is undoubtedly a very interesting shamanic journey.

It is a relatively safe journey too; I sincerely believe that anyone can do it following a few basic guidelines. You don't need to have a drum or maracas. You can use a recording from Youtube or a CD, although I particularly like to play for myself. It's also a challenge, making the journey while you're playing. You don't totally abandon consciousness while playing and trying not to lose the rhythm while you try to cross the veil to another plane, but it can be done. In fact, I also do it when I am taking another person to the other side, to travel at the same time, to accompany them and see if I can see something else for them.

To make this journey, if you do not have much experience, I recommend you start by preparing the space. It may sound silly but it is very important. I'm not just talking about clearing energy or creating sacred space according to your tradition. That the location is moderately in order, will contribute to order or balance in your experience and this is applicable to any pre-ritual or magical preparation. Once the space is ready and you have created a sacred space, if you do not have a power animal, it does not matter, because they will not participate in the experience. If you do, call them, so that they can support you on an energetic level. Call your guides also if you wish, so that they support you during the experience. Do not forget to leave offerings for your ancestors on the altar, also leave something for the spirits of the place and the land you are going to visit. The intention is to connect not only with the ancestors, but also with the land.

We know that places are impregnated with experiences and energies. Perhaps this is easier to check in a house, because of the limited size, the energies are concentrated in a certain way. We know that water has memory, we know that we can program, for example, objects or crystals with magical or energetic intentions precisely because of their ability to store information. When we are outdoors, the same thing happens. The energy varies a lot from one place to another, not only because of the polarity of its invisible beings, but also because of the weight of the memories of events that happened there. The intention for this journey is to connect with the land and try to get the place or invisible beings or guardians of the place to share with us a memory of our ancestors. This can happen in several ways, these are three of them, although there are more:

1. Through a body of water, for example, when approaching a body of water in that determined place, we could be shown a vision in the water.
2. The memories emanate from the place as if they were a hologram of the past and can show us events in relation to our ancestors.
3. We will be able to see our ancestors as invisible witnesses and see how they relate with that place.

Remember that you have to make the intention of the work clear throughout the process, make a kind of declaration of intentions, because this is what is going to program the experience. At different times throughout the journey it is important that in our head, we repeat the intention of the journey and in some way, we can also ask our ancestors and the place and spirits of the place to help us see. We do not journey in the shamanic worlds simply as tourists — through this journey we can understand the past of our ancestors and therefore better understand ourselves, knowing that their lives affect ours in one way or another. It can also help you understand connections. So no, it's not a recreational journey, I don't believe in recreational journeys to shamanic worlds, I think that you always have to enter with an intention that can bring healing for you or for others.

So, now I am going to give you a map with the steps to follow to make this shamanic journey. You will have to memorise it and be clear about the key points, because you will need to do your journey with the drum and follow it remembering those steps for the journey. We are going to start this shamanic journey by going into the forest. Remember to keep the intention in your mind along the way. We walk for a few minutes to find our way through the trees until we reach a clearing. In that clearing we are going to see a big tree; we are going to get closer. It is a robust and tall tree, so tall that we can see how its trunk reaches into the clouds. Right now, we have to climb the tree, little by little. We know that in the shamanic worlds, time is elastic, in reality it will only take you a few minutes to climb to the top. You will literally find yourself walking on top of the clouds. Let's go find the edge of the cloud.

At this point your intention has to be more than expressed, therefore everything is left to the spirits and ancestors. When you get to the edge of the cloud, lean out because below is the place we have to visit. At this point you will have to throw yourself into the void, but don't be scared, the shamanic worlds are somehow also a bit like dreams. You will reach solid ground as if you had only taken a slight jump.

It may happen that when we arrive, we do not see anyone. You can ask where you arc, the spirits of the place usually answer. If you don't see any body of water nearby, wait a few more minutes until your ancestor appears or the place shows you the memory. If someone appears, surely it is your ancestor. Remember that it can be any ancestor of any time in the history of one of your two bloodlines. Typically, we do not know who it is. Just watch and listen until the drum tells you it's time to go back. When this happens, say goodbye with respect or thanks to the spirits and the place for what has been shown to you in one way or another. To return you will only have to stomp your feet on the ground and you will be back in the cloud, look for the branches of the tree and go down it. Leave the forest clearing and return. This is the end of your journey.

Bone Magic in Ancient Times

Looking for magic in antiquity, we would have to start our search in the Near East. The oldest magic that we are going to find is in clay tablets, in cuneiform writing. The Greek philosophers told us about the Zoroastrian Magus or Magi of Persia and the necromantic practices that came to Greece from the East.

Although most of the great philosophers, including those of the Pythagorean school, would end up bearing the title of Magus, the very practices of the physicians of the time would not be far removed from magical practices. Interestingly, we are going to find a lot of magic in literature starting with Homer's Odyssey, going through works by Lucan, Apuleius, Virgil, Ovid, Horace and Theocritus.

We find among literary texts necromantic practices, love spells and curses. We also find that in Greco Roman necromantic practices there is a group of deities that are commonly mentioned in magical spells and incantations. These deities are Hecate, Hades/Pluto, Persephone, Mercury, Charon, Chaos, Circe, the

Fates, Styx, the Furies, and also Demogorgon. And we will find magical references of popular characters such as Medea, Circe and the witches Erichtho, Pamphile and Meroe. Next, we will review some of these classic texts.

Binding spell: Simaetha's erotic magic to recover the errant Delphis

This is a binding spell that was composed by the poet Theocritus. We find a lot of incantations in literature and this is a fine example. Delivered as a monologue, the spell caster is Simaetha, who wishes to attract a certain individual, Delphi, her object of desire. In this spell Simaetha replaces Delphi's bones with barley grains, that is why I have decided to include part of it as an example of sympathetic magic. This is an extract from the Idyll 2 from Theocritus:

> Where did I put my bay leaves? Fetch them, Thestylis. Where are my love potions [philtra] Garland the bowl with crimson sheep's wool, so that I may bind [katadesomai] my dear man, who is unkind to me. The miserable man has not even visited me for eleven days, nor does he know whether I am alive or dead. Nor has he knocked at my door, the hateful one. Eros and Aphrodite have gone off, taking his flighty mind with them. I'll go to Timagetus's wrestling gym tomorrow to see him, and I'll reproach him for his treatment of me. But now I will bind him with sacrifices. Moon, shine brightly. For I shall sing gently to you, goddess, and to chthonic Hecate, at whom even the dogs tremble as she comes across the tombs of the dead and the black blood. Welcome, frightful Hecate, and accompany me to the completion of my task. Render these drugs no less powerful that those of Circe, Medea, or blonde Perimede.
>
> Wryneck [iunx], draw this man to my house. First, barley-grains disintegrate in the fire. But sprinkle them on, Thestylis. Poor woman, have you lost your mind? Sprinkle them, and while you do it say this: "I sprinkle the bones of Delphis."

Wryneck, draw this man to my house. Delphis has caused me pain. I burn this bay leaf against Delphis. And as this bay leaf is set alight, crackles loudly in the flames, and quickly blazes up, leaving no ash for us to see, so may Delphis too shrivel his flesh in the flames.

Wryneck, draw this man to my house. Now I will sacrifice the bran. You, Artemis, could move even the adamant in Hades and anything else difficult to shift. Thestylis, the dogs howl in the city. The goddess is at the crossroads. Sound the bronze as quickly as possible.

Wryneck, draw this man to my house. See, the sea is silent, silent the breezes. But the pain within my breast is not silent. I am ablaze over him who has made me a wretched, wicked, despicable nonvirgin, instead of a wife.

Wryneck, draw this man to my house. As I melt this wax doll with the help of the goddess, so may Delphis of Myndos at once be melted by love. And as by the power of Aphrodite this bronze bull-roarer [rhombos] whirls round, so may he whirl round at my door.

Some Spells from the PGM as found on the Greek Magical Papyri in Translation edited by Hans Dieter Betz.

Amulet to Ward off Ghosts:

You will need a large Hyena tooth. Carried with you, tied on a cord, it prevents night terrors and ghosts.

Charm to induce insomnia:

[Take] a seashell and write: i "IPSAE IAOAI, let her, NN daughter of NN, lie awake because of me." That night she will lie awake.

An Amulet:

Wear a wolf knucklebone, mix juice of vetch and of pondweed in a censer, write in the middle of the censer this name:

'HERMOUTHEREPSIPHIRIPHI PISALI" (24 letter). And in this way make an offering.

A Love Spell of Attraction:

Offering to the star of Aphrodite: A white dove's blood and fat, untreated myrrh and parched wormwood. Make this up together as pills and offer them to the star on pieces of vine wood or on coals. And also have the brains of a vulture for the compulsion, so that you may make the offering. And also have as a protective charm a tooth from the upper right jawbone of a female ass or of a tawny sacrificial heifer, tied to your left arm with I Anuhian thread.

Another Love Spell of Attraction

Purify yourself from everything for days and say [this] spell at sunrise: "Helios . . . but come here to me, [Mistress AKTIOPHIS ERESCHIGAL] PERSEPHONE; I attract [to me and bind her], NN, whom NN bore, [to] the man who is [pining away] with [passion for her]; at this very moment, inflame her that she fulfil the nightly desires of NN, whom NN bore. Aye, lord NETHMOMAO [Helios, enter] into the [soul] of her, NN, whom NN bore, I and [burn her heart], her guts, [her liver, her spirit, her bones. Perform] successfully for me [this] charm, immediately, immediately; [quickly, quickly]."

Some of My Spells with Bones

A protection spell working with the spirit of the badger
Badgers are very special animals. When we think of protection, people usually think of dogs, but in nature there are animals that are incredibly protective of their territory and home, the badger is one of them. Such is their power that it is one of my favourite animals to work with shamanically, especially to help

other people. Badger is great to help people struggling to set boundaries and their space is continually invaded or they feel like they are bullied by others.

This is a very effective spell to protect spaces, not only from invasions on this plane, but also from magical attacks. I have a variant to protect people that I am going to share separately.

In order to perform this spell, I recommend working with either the badger's jaw or skull, or with a claw or paw. Unfortunately, quite a few badgers are hit by cars, so it is possible to find people who sell badger bones or skins that have been rescued from accidents. If you don't want to work with any part of the animal, you can use a figure to represent them, although the energy will be different.

For this work as in any other, offerings are important. We can leave food offerings or somehow feed the spirit of the badger while it is helping us. Another way to make your offering to the badger is, for example, to help an association that protects them.

We are going to take a cloth bag or a glass jar. They do not have to be very big, the intention is to hang them or to be able to leave them near our door. In the bag or jar we are going to deposit the badger's jaw or claw together with some protecting herbs. Actually, this is all we need. But if we want, we can even create a reduction sigil that mentions the badger.

If you work with crystals there are several crystals that are protective and you could also include them. The easiest to find is black tourmaline, but a jet crystal would also be very suitable. We can include a pentagram or other protective symbols, even a small mirror or piece of mirror. When we have the bag or jar ready, we will recite the following:

My fierce badger friend, hear my call, accept my offerings. Help me protect my home from threats, from strangers and acquaintances with evil intentions, that anyone who dares to enter or invade my home or tries to use other means including technology or magic to harm me or my people, may suffer the pain of your piercing fangs in their flesh, may your claws tear apart their ill intentions. May they see their evil returned and multiplied.

Place the bag at your front door or at the entrance of your property. If you are going to place it outdoors, it is better to use the glass jar. While you have this protection activated, remember to renew your offerings. When you want to disable this protection, thank the Badger for helping you and place the badger bone back inside to rest.

Personal protection badger amulet

To create this amulet, we are going to use a badger claw or tooth. We can put it inside a medicine bag hanging from your neck or carry it as a keychain.

We will start with our offerings before we carry the bone with us. To activate the protective spell, we will say the following:

My fierce badger friend, listen to my call, accept my offerings. Help me protect myself from threats, from strangers and acquaintances with bad intentions, remove from my path all evil, all malicious obstacles, any person or situation that represents a threat or danger for my well-being throughout my day.

Take this amulet with you wherever you want to go or when you prepare to travel. To deactivate it, thank the badger and leave a final offering, remove the badger bone and let it rest.

Spell for protection working with Hecate

This spell can be used as a base to work with any animal you work with. You only need a bone or skeleton and do not forget that some animals have an exoskeleton.

For this protection spell we are going to use a dog bone and if it is the skull even better, since we are also going to work with Hecate and the dark moon.

You Need:

Dog bone
Black, red and white candles
Offerings for Hecate: Olive oil, Garlic and Poppies
A black cotton Cloth
Broken glass
You can also prepare garlic oil, you just have to peel the garlic and make a cut and put them in olive oil for a week

On the Dark Moon, prepare the altar with the offerings and the candles. On the black cloth, place the dog bone. We are going to consecrate the bone, for this we are going to anoint it with garlic oil or olive oil and sprinkle the poppy petals on it. Next, we are going to add the broken glass, please be careful not to cut yourself.

We are going to raise our hands in a supplicating position and say:

Hecate, Lykania, Apotropaia, Kynegetis! Accept my offerings, hear my prayer! May your dogs protect my home from harm! May they stand guard over me and my blood. May their jaws tear out the flesh of my enemies, may their bark keep those with ill intention at bay.

Close the cloth and keep it on your altar until the candles go out. You will have to find a place inside your property boundaries to bury the bone, preferably near a main door, front or back.

Spell to attract money and abundance

For this spell you need:

    1 lucky chicken bone
    3 Copper Coins or similar alloy
    1 Pyrite Crystal
    1 Key
    Seeds
    flowers
    Green tissue paper or cloth

We will clean the chicken bone. On the tissue paper or green cloth, we are going to deposit the bone, the seeds, the three coins, the pyrite crystal, the key and the flowers. We make a small package with it and while holding it we will recite three times:

I bring the magic of abundance into my life, with beauty and harmony. May my door open to prosperity, may a shower of blessings flow through it.

Bury your parcel next to Daffodils that receive direct rainwater. It can also be a planter outside.

Another abundance spell using fishbones

This is a spell inspired by a fairy tale that my mother used to tell me when I was little.

For this spell we will need the complete skeleton of a fish, it does not matter if it is marine or river fish. If you can fish for it yourself all the better, but you can also buy it. In Spain we eat a lot of fish and it is easy to find whole fresh fish in the local fishmongers or in the supermarket. Where I live in Scotland it is more difficult to find whole fresh fish from the sea, or they sell the fillets without bones. Personally, when I buy fish at the fishmonger, I honour it just as if I had caught it myself. In this case it is already dead, sometimes the fish ends up in the bin if it is not sold and that really makes me feel sorrier than eating it with honour. Since I was a child, I used to hunt octopus. I did it with my own hands, diving. I fished with my hands, for me it was a fair fight, in which I had to fight, almost out of breath at times. When I ate those octopuses, I honoured them, as intelligent and strong adversaries. I haven't caught octopus in a long time, but I still honour them, even if I buy them. And I do the same with the rest of the fish or shellfish. I integrate the energy of the sea in me through them. Of course, if we buy wild fish, it is much better.

For this spell you will need:

A complete fish skeleton
A copper or silver coin for each main spine of the skeleton and one for the mouth
Poppy seeds and other seeds
A Gold or Yellow candle
Loose rice
Yellow flowers
Bay leaves
Cinnamon stick or ground
Green or purple tissue paper
Wool or natural Greek cotton thread
Natural incense
Golden sugar and/or honey

Perhaps the easiest way to get fish bones is by making a fish soup. Of course, try to remove the flesh before the skeleton breaks. If you break off the head when handling it, it's okay, try to put it together during preparation. Once our bones are clean, we're going to set them aside. We are going to take the tissue paper and we are going to put it open on the table. Let's prepare the base, actually it's a bit like making a mandala. We will make a bed of rice and seeds, then we will put our yellow flower petals around it and the bay leaves. Sprinkle the cinnamon, either powdered or in small pieces. Now it's time to place the fish on top of our mandala on the paper, in the centre. Place the coins more or less matching the main bones and remember to put one in the mouth, if it can't be inside, place it outside. Take a few minutes and light your incense. Look at that mandala of flowers, seeds and bones. If you need abundance for any specific reason, talk to the fish. You don't need a spell itself, but if we are going to ask for help, to give us abundance, we can also write a small prayer on a piece of paper, asking for help. If you write it on a piece of paper, when you're done, you'll have to fold it and place it under the fish. When we have finished making our spoken or written requests, we are going to take the Golden Sugar and we are going to sprinkle it on top of our mandala. Adding sweetness to work, so that the abundance or money we need comes without pain.

Now we will proceed to create a small parcel with our mandala inside. We are going to close the paper over the mandala carefully and we will use the wool or cotton cord to close the package. Don't worry, it's normal for it to move when you close it, that's why meditation and intention time is important before closing it. We will take our package and bury it in the garden, not too deep. That's why we have to make sure that all the material is biodegradable. Once we deposit our parcel in the ground, it takes a few minutes. You can improvise something like:

Mother Earth, I give you this offering of abundance, so that you multiply it with your blessings. May the seeds flourish and abundance bathe my home. I declare myself a prosperous daughter of the earth.

When you're done, cover it with soil and water it generously. Remember to water it regularly.

Spell with seagull bone to achieve a purpose or something specific

This spell is conceived to work with the spirit of the Seagull, to help us achieve a purpose or mission or to help us to get something specific and tangible.

The reason why I work with the seagull and not another animal is more than obvious. They are tenacious animals, they are very intelligent, cunning and they almost always get all they want. Their survival instinct makes them fierce when it comes to getting what they want. If you have ever seen seagulls fighting for their food you will know this. Seagulls are a bit like the winged foxes of the sea. The seagulls are going to help us using all their resources, they are opportunistic and persevering like nobody else when they want something. Plus they are fast and imposing, they have attitude — we cannot deny this. As a magical ally, they are magnificent.

To perform this spell you will need:

A seagull bone (if you can source one)
A shell or hag stone
Beach elements for your altar
A glass bottle with a cork
A seagull feather
Driftwood
Paper
Ink
Food offerings for the seagulls

Sometimes you can find seagull bones on the beach, I found mine there. You will have to create an altar for the seagulls.

You can easily do it with things you find on the beach. There are always many seagull feathers. If you don't have a bone, you can also just use a feather. This is the easiest option for many people, but if you find a bone it's much better.

Depending on what you want to get through the seagull, you will have to maintain the altar and make offerings for three months, three weeks or three days. You can make offerings to the seagulls that you have nearby, feeding them. This is a very easy way to establish a relationship with them while the spirit of the seagull is helping you. I had a seagull friend that I fed. She would come and sit in the kitchen window, until I saw her and went out to feed her. She came almost every day and the truth is that although at that time I did not feed her with magical intentions, the connection was established and that was what gave origin to this spell.

When it comes to time, it all depends on how much time you have and also, as I said, what you want to achieve. If you have lost something or want something more trivial or small, three days is enough. If it is something urgent, even if it is more important, you can always at least do those three days if you have them. We will make our offerings for three weeks or three months if we need the seagull to bring us something more complicated, if it depends on more people or a group. For example, if you want to change jobs, or a new job, or need income, we will ask the seagull to bring us coins. Something that she could pick up with her beak physically. The same if we want a new house, we will ask the seagull to bring us a key. You can, of course, ask her to bring you the house that is most suitable for you, to bring you the keys to your ideal house.

You can work with seagulls in general or if you know a particular seagull, you can focus on it. As we have a seagull feather or bone, we can also address the spirit of the seagull to which the bone or feather belonged. When we know what we want to ask the seagull, we will proceed as follows:

1. We will prepare the altar with things that we have collected on the beach. Gulls live inland too, but the sea is their habitat.
2. On our altar, we will have to deposit a shell or a hag stone. We will have to speak to the spirit of the seagull through the hole in the stone or through the shell and remind the seagull what you need. You can do this on the days you feed the seagulls that you have nearby, later, never before. You can even write a short prayer for the seagull and recite it this way.
3. To leave a message to the seagull about what we want, we will need a transparent glass bottle or a jar. We will write our message on a piece of paper, if you want you can write it with the seagull feather and ink. Once we have reflected what we need on the paper, we will put it inside the bottle and close it with a cork. We will leave our bottle and its message on the altar until what we have asked of the seagull materialises. After this we can take out the paper and burn it in a small fire that we will make with wood from the beach if we can, at least using a stick found near the sea. We can deliver the ashes to the sea as a way to close the job. 4. Finally, leave an offering to the seagulls.

If you don't want to stop working with them, simply continue making your offerings and proceed in the same way, putting your want/need in the bottle.

Spell to achieve a purpose working with the fox spirit

This is a spell designed to help us achieve something that requires extra cunning and audacity. For this we are going to work with the fox. Who better than him to help us? You can use this spell when there is also a legal process involved or you have to get something through paperwork.

The fox usually has a bad reputation in the wild animal bestiary, but humans are to blame for this. The fox is nothing more than an animal that strives for what it wants and that unfortunately has been displaced and its natural space reduced by the growth of cities or land and farms. Now more and more urban foxes are seen, which have had to adapt or struggle to survive between concrete and humans, often searching for food in the garbage.

The fox is a cunning survivor, who knows how to act in the most complicated situations. He acts quickly and with determination, he is an effective animal — for that reason we are going to work with him.

Our offering to the fox when we need his help is going to be food, things that he can hunt to eat. For example, we can offer rabbit, chicken meat, also a little fresh cream mixed with beaten egg, fresh eggs, chicken eggs or quail eggs. We can offer them seasonal fruits and forest berries. We can make a protective offering for the fox, helping an organisation that fights to protect them.

For this spell we are going to prepare an altar that we will maintain until what we need is achieved.

For our altar we will need:

A fox bone, any bone, doesn't have to be the skull or you can use other parts of the fox, its skin would work too
Candles
A box or jar to store the intention of the work
Food offerings for the fox

You can put wild flowers on the altar, and other elements that you have found in nature.

We have to be very clear that we need the fox. We are going to write what we need on the paper and we will keep it in the box or jar. We can also create a reduction sigil that includes the fox. If the fox bone we have is small, you can keep it with the request, if it is bigger or it is, for example, a fox tail, you can place it on top of the request.

When our altar is ready, we will proceed to call the spirit of the fox:

Fox, on this day I send a call for help. I need your cunning, your agility and your senses to be able to resolve this matter. My dear fox, help me to get what I need, go through the resistances, find a way, help me avoid obstacles, take what I need and bring it to me, avoid my enemies if there are any, don't let them achieve their purpose, help me escape if necessary. You are faster, more cunning, more resourceful than anyone. Share with me the greatness of your magic, Fox help me and together we will celebrate.

When the fox gets what you need, don't forget to leave him a good offering.

Candle to Honour the Goddess Agrona

We are going to create an Offering Candle for the Scottish Goddess Agrona, also called Aeron. This Goddess is the Genius Loci of the River Ayr and the Sovereign Goddess of the county of Ayrshire, the former Kingdom of Aeron. Although some people just know her as a Goddess related to battle, of slaughter and carnage, she is far more complex than that. To me, because of my personal experience with her, she is a very ancient deity, linked to death but also to life. Agrona being a Goddess of the land and the soil in Ayrshire being so rich, she is abundant. It is her fertile soil that feeds the crops, she is fertile. But she is also a Goddess of livestock, especially cattle and horses. Her very name gives origin to the word agriculture, so that is very significant. She feeds the people that work her land. Ayrshire is also very rich in minerals and has a very important mining industry. So, she is clearly, at least to me, a harvest and life giving deity. But I also see her relationship to death, and I feel that she is fiercely protective of her land, a battle Goddess. Agrona, like The Morrigan is linked to the crow, I always see them around her in my visions of her. She is also a washer Goddess. In the last vision I had of her, she had her feet in the water, she carried a spear, but she also had a sword and a shield. I saw she had some sort of short cape over her shoulders, made of what seemed like cow hide but with longer hair. I also saw crow feathers, maybe in her hair from what I remember, and she had a cow horn. Somehow, I have the feeling of Agrona being close both to Brigantia and The Morrigan.

The presence of the Goddess is imposing in the lands that she governs, especially in the Cumnock area, towards Muirkirk, or coming from Darvel towards the same area. Just there, in between, we will find the place from which she emanates, on the border with South Lanarkshire. The area is totally liminal. Even modern places around hold the name Nether. This is a personal perception: somehow her energy extends to the Irvine Valley as well, from the Muirkirk area. I'm still trying to find out more about the Irvine River but my feeling is that Agrona emanates from this land in between both rivers. Maybe these rivers are her arms embracing the county physically with her waters. But then she is said to also manifest in the Aeron River in Wales.

To create this devotional candle for Agrona we are going to need beef marrow fat. We can get fresh cow bones with marrow; I usually buy the bones to make broth at my local butcher and they are also found in some supermarkets. I have even seen online shops that sell bone marrow. We can melt the marrow fat and filter it, if you wish. You can also make broth with the bones and let it cool down. You're going to have a bunch of marrow fat on top of the pot, pretty much clean. I have made broth many times but I did not remember the fat, a friend reminded me. Once filtered, we will mix it with the beeswax.

When the mixture is still hot, we can add some small pebbles from the River Ayr or Aeron. You can also add some grass or herbs from a local moorland or hill too. Instead of using a metal or glass container for our candle, we can use a hollow cow bone as a container for our wax. We can close it with a cork or limpet shell as I did myself. You can use the candle once it cools down, but wait at least 24 hours. I would also wait for the dark moon to offer this candle. When you are ready, place the candle in the altar and proceed to do your offering. I was told in a vision that we can also use the flame of the candle to meditate and we might be presented with a vision or information.

Protective Candle Dedicated to Hestia

We are going to work with Hestia in this spell because there is no one better than her to protect the home and our family. Hestia is a Titan, the elder sister of Zeus, Poseidon and Hades. She is the protector of the Fire, the Home, the Family and the Hearth. That makes her a good deity to entrust our family to. Her purifying aspect will increase the cleansing intentions and power of our candle at an energetic level. Furthermore, she is also related to Delphi, so we can also include divination to some degree, by observing at the candle flame.

To create this candle you will need:

Teeth or pieces of teeth, either yours or any of your children or ancestors if you have any. (We all lose teeth when we are children or maybe you have had a tooth removed! After the candle is consumed you can recover it anyway)
Bee wax. Since one of Hestia's sacred animals is the pig, you could include some Lard to honour her

Rosemary and Chaste Tree berries or flowers. Dried leaves are good too. Even powdered
A veil to cover your head

Offerings: you can offer her things that are usually found in the kitchen, oil, animal fat to cook, honey. Of course, if you cook pork for her, it will be very well received.

We are going to create our candle, of course, you always have to be very careful with the hot wax. Let's add the plants. Finally, we will add the tooth.

Once the candle cools down, I recommend waiting at least 24 hours before we use it so the elements and energy of the candle settles a bit. When we are ready, we can go burn it, we will seal the intention of this candle by saying the following:

Hestia Goddess of the Hearth, you who represent purification, I light this candle to ask for protection for my family, may this flame dissipate the shadows hovering over us, may its light blind those who direct their evil gaze towards us, may your fire consume the negative energies that may be acting against us. Powerful Hestia, accept my humble offerings, keep my family, my bones safe, let us remain under your protection.

You can repeat this spell and offering once a month if you wish, so you maintain continuous protection.

Crow dance in honour of Agrona and the Morrigan

This is an offering dance. You can use it to honour the Raven Goddesses, the Scottish Goddess Agrona — Aeron or the popular The Morrigan. These two goddesses are closely related. Of course, you can use it to honour other goddesses who are also related to corvids.

You can perform this dance in front of your altar or outdoors, you can also include it as part of a larger ritual. The idea is to channel the energy of the crow and the goddesses through the dance. The essentials for this dance are two raven wings, although you can also make a raven mask to wear during the dance as an extra. You need to dress completely in black, if you don't have the mask you will have to cover your head with a black chiffon veil. You don't need background music, the idea is to flow with the energy, of course, if you are going to do this as part of a larger ritual or to do it in public you could use some Celtic music or bagpipes, but it is better to avoid a fast tempo, the chosen music should be slow.

We will take the two wings in our hands and the idea is to imitate the crows, both in their walk and in their flight. If you don't know how to do it, or you don't see them often, you can watch videos of crows to help you find movements of the animal to combine with dance.

Sea Oracle

For those people who like me are passionate about the sea and water, we are going to create a marine oracle. We are going to find absolutely all the elements that we need on the beach. Conches, shells, pieces of driftwood, seaglass, stones — sometimes we even find rusty bits of metal or nuts and seeds. I have also found bones on the beach. Not everything you find has to be marine in that sense. The beach offers us many elements to be able to create an oracle. When the tide is low it is an ideal time to search for items.

When it comes to how many pieces you need, it's really hard to say. You always have to start with something we can handle — if you start with too many pieces you can find it difficult. Better to start with less than 15 items. Once you gain practice you can increase the number. You can, for example, use conches to represent people, age differences too. You have to choose a piece that represents you, you need another that represents obstacles or problems, one that represents the couple, it can be a limpet ring, I find them on the beach all the time, find one that also represents your home. It's not a bad idea to include something that represents money or economy, you can use a sand dollar for it, also include something that represents luck for you, if you find a tiny starfish on the shore that is dead you could use it. Sometimes I find dead crabs or crab claws. These can be used to represent enemies, although in some cultures they bring good luck too. Sea Urchins could also represent enemies or difficult situations. Make sure you also introduce elements of time, something to mark time in some way. Present and future, past also if you wish.

The first thing is to find your elements, then you can dedicate yourself to assigning meanings. Also, where you keep them is very important. It can be a bag or a box. Think that if you are going to be using them often it will have to be something that you can transport easily. When you have your oracle ready, it is time to present it to your ancestors. This type of oracle works very well in connection with our ancestors, to establish a means of communication with them, but I know of people who dedicate their oracles to deities. You can do what you like, one option is not better than the other.

Once you have done the presentation to your ancestors or deities and consecration of your oracle, you can start using it. Whenever you are going to take a reading, it is necessary to establish protection elements and, of course, clean the space as much as possible. Once you gain more practice with your oracle and do readings for other people, cleaning the oracle itself will also be very important. Although it also happens with the tarot, organic oracles collect more energy. They are also much more complex readings so you don't want remnants of a previous reading in someone else's oracle.

Another way to add depth to your reading is to create reading templates. Although the truth is that I do not recommend using them from the beginning, since in some way they will affect your interpretation and you will not make an effort to establish a deeper connection. You can trace the templates as you like, I personally used concentric circles in the past. Four concentric circles on a piece of white cloth. Each of them has a specific aspect. You can make any pattern of your liking, a pyramid or divide the template into quadrants. From experience, more than four separations can be chaotic, but try and experiment. This oracle above all is yours, it is your creation. Flow and learn with each reading.

Marine Protection Ritual

You can use this ritual to protect someone during a journey or you can use it to raise a general shield of protection. It can be reinforced with several elements to extend the protection.

We use the limpet because I know very few molluscs as hard as this one. I don't know if you've seen them in their natural environment or have ever caught limpets, but it's very hard to catch them. They stick to rocks like cement. That is why they are ideal for creating a sea magical shield.

For the basic spell you need:

A blue candle
Sea salt
Beach sand
Powdered dried seaweed
13 + 1 limpets
Urchin Spines
Sea urchin (optional)
A bowl
Paper

We will take the candle and consecrate it with a little natural oil. Then we will sprinkle it with salt, sand and powdered algae and put it in a bowl that will also have sand from the beach. Next, we will write the name of the person we want to protect on the paper and we will put the paper inside one of the limpets and we will put it in the bowl facing down with the paper inside. Then we will place the other 13 barnacles around the bowl. We will light our candle and drop a few drops of blue wax on the limpet in the bowl saying:

By this spell, the person whose name is on this paper, comes under the protection of the ocean and its creatures.

We can reinforce this protection to fight against magic or malicious attacks, using sea urchin spines or small crabs or crab claws between the limpets of the circle by adding:

May the person who dares to raise a finger or magic word against this person, find obstacles and problems until they desist from their evil intentions.

We will let the candle burn completely and repeat if we see it necessary after a few weeks.

If we feel attacked or we are clearly being intentionally attacked on this reality or through magic, we can use the same spell and say this when we place the sea urchin spines on the altar:

May the person or persons, known or unknown, who are behind this personal, physical or/and magical attack not be able to reach me or touch me, may their poisoned words dissolve into the sea, so they stop causing harm, may their malicious actions be reversed, from today the spirit of the sea urchin protects me. The urchin spirit returns with intense pain, their attempts to reach me, I am protected.

Or, we can perform the spell by substituting the barnacle in the centre for a sea urchin with its spikes. We will place our name or the person to defend inside the urchin and we will repeat those same words.

Ritual to Attract Love

For this ritual we are going to work with the energy of the deer. Because for me the deer represents one of the main energies of love in the forest, unconditional love, family, and strength to fight for your loved ones, also to protect them. So, this spell is ideal for a person who wants to find a partner to start a family. If what you want is a sexual partner, there are other animals with which we can work, the deer would not be the most suitable.

For this spell we need:

The deer antler whistle
Fresh grass and fruit. You can even germinate your grass
yourself
Forest elements for our altar. Like dry leaves, pine cones,
forest fruits, etc.
A pillar candle
Musky perfume
Symbols that represent love for you

Although we can perform this spell from the time deer begin rutting, in autumn, until the season ends, there is another auspicious date for this spell, the deer full moon or buck moon in July. You can actually do this spell for love and family from that day and do it every full moon if you wish.

After having purified ourselves, we will prepare our altar with the offerings, the loving symbols and our candle. We can even find a heart-shaped box to store our deer whistle. When our altar is ready, we will light the candle and take a few minutes to meditate on our desires to find a partner. Next, we will put on the musk perfume and say or read aloud:

Sweet, sweet deer, sweet-eyed prince of the forest. Accept these gifts. Hear the prayer of this human who opens his/her heart to you to find love. Share your stamina, persistence and strength with me. May your call also be mine somehow. Help me attract a mate, so we can celebrate spring together. Sweet, sweet deer, loving is your call and the forest awakens to love with you. Take my call to the right person for me, one to build a happy home with. May my call reach the one that is perfect for me.

Then take your whistle and blow in full awareness, knowing that your call can be heard. While you whistle is a good time to connect, as you are blowing, your breathing is altered and you may enter a trance state. If a vision comes to you at this time, pay attention to the details, you can be given clues so when you finish, try to take notes. Store the whistle in its heart-shaped box or wherever you wish to store it. Thank the deer spirit for its help and let the candle burn down completely. Repeat your ritual again as instructed during the rutting season.

Brooch Amulet to Attract a Lover

If we are not interested in attracting a partner as such, but we want to attract a lover into our life, we can work with the pheasant as a spiritual ally to achieve it. You may not know it but the pheasant is an animal famous for having a very high libido. To the point that he is not limited to having one partner — it is not uncommon for the male pheasant to share his charms with up to three females at the same time. The pheasant is also a very striking and attractive bird. Its colours really attract attention, especially its red head and tail. The pheasant is truly flamboyant. So, working with its energy is going to help us get the attention of the opposite sex, and the pheasant also helps us with its audacity and stamina. The pheasant can also help us to leave the past behind and take a step forward for new goals, not only in the sexual sense, but also in other areas of our lives. As you can see, the magical work with pheasants is more than interesting! This spell is very specific but we can work more things with his help. For example, it can also help us if for some reason we wish to stand out or if we have to be noticed or chosen for something. The pheasant will also help us in these situations. Pheasants fly, even if it is a limited distance — but it is the energy of that explosive jump and short flight, that impulse that is going to help us.

To work magically with the energy of the pheasant we are going to create a magical amulet to attract a lover. We can take this amulet whenever we have plans to attend a social event and we want to take advantage of the occasion to attract someone.

To create this amulet we are going to need:

Pheasant feathers with some red or orange colour (natural, not dyed)

A Pheasant foot or bone. (If you wish to add a little extra energy)

Felt and tweed fabric in similar shades

A piece of cardboard or wood panel in the shape of a heart

Safety pin or brooch pin

Hot glue gun or quick glue just in case

Dried flowers. You can add dry herbs from the field

A cotton ball

Of course, you can choose to do it your way, this is just an example. You are going to make a pretty mini bouquet with the feathers and the dried flowers. You are going to partially wrap it with tweed fabric, you can also use ribbon, it has to look pretty. Use the glue gun or quick glue to seal the fabric and dry the feathers and flowers, so they don't get loose. Next, we are going to cover our wooden heart with felt or tweed. We're going to put some cotton on top of the wood for a little padding. You will need to have cut a felt heart of the same size as the wood to glue on the back, to which you will have also previously sewn the pin. You should have glued the tweed from the part that is visible to the back, so that it stays tight. Glue the heart-shaped felt with the pin on the back. A stitch here and there will help to keep the two parts together stronger. Once you have lined the heart, let the glue dry. Now we can glue and sew our bouquet on top. It's better if we glue it and then we give it a few stitches to make sure it won't come loose.

For this amulet you can just use the feathers because they are very striking, but you can make the bouquet with a small pheasant bone if you wish or even with a pheasant's foot as well, these are easy to find online if you don't know a hunter.

Cornucopia Magic for Abundance

You may have seen a goddess holding a cornucopia. Sometimes I include the cornucopia on my altar to bring abundant energy into my ritual. For my cornucopia I use a goat's horn that my son found in the mountains. Goats are animals that have accompanied humans since ancient times, giving us their milk and their meat. Having a goat is a blessing in some way, so I prefer goat horns, but you can use another type of horn. Bulls and cows have also been associated with abundance, so you might as well use their horns if you wish. To put inside your horn: Acorns, various seeds, including poppy seeds. Dry fruit, like dates, although I also try to use grapes or raisins. I like to use grapes because we always see them in classical cornucopia representations, but if you are going to use them fresh, use them at the end, to kind of close the cornucopia, and make sure they don't rot inside the horn. I also like to include grain in my cornucopia, either wheat or barley and I put silver coins and copper coins in too. I like to use some flowers, to add a touch of beauty energy. We can share the abundant energy of this cornucopia with others if we want to by inserting pieces of paper with the names of the people to whom we want to send abundant energy and blessings. This is a great thing to do for a harvest celebration in a group and include the name of the people attending your sabbat or ritual. We will leave offerings on the altar, we will also offer incense and we can light some beeswax candles. Of course, we can invoke some Goddesses as part of our ritual, such as Fortuna, Ceres, Demeter or Abundantia, although you can do something more neutral without dedicating your horn to any deity. When you finish stuffing your horn, take it with both hands and raise it saying:

I thank Mother Earth for her abundance that is represented in this horn of plenty. Mother Earth, let this horn be a recipient of your generosity, which never ceases. Mother, you who multiply everything we give you, who makes each seed flourish. Accept my offerings, may this Cornucopia be your manifestation of abundance and creatrix energy on my altar and in my house.

Place the cornucopia on the altar and continue with the ritual. You can also invite people to place their offering in the altar now, if you are holding a public ritual and you might change the wording slightly at the end as:

May this Cornucopia be your manifestation of abundance and creatrix energy on this altar and for everyone present here today.

Magical Incenses with Bones

We can make incense in a traditional way in a mortar or if you prefer, use a manual or electric spice or coffee grinder. The grinder is great for getting fine textures. We need the grinder to crush the bones to turn them into powder if you don't want to do it by hand in the mortar. We are in the technological age, there is nothing wrong with making use of this technology if you wish to use an electric grinder! If you want to make your own incense cones or sticks, I recommend you grind everything a little more, so that later you can add a little distilled water (just a few drops), honey or other sticky stuff. This will help to work the mix and then let the cones dry. I do not mention amounts as I normally play by ear when it comes to magical mixing, also when it comes to cooking! My grandmother never used a kitchen scale and in Granada we actually have a special way to measure things. Even if you go shopping you can ask for a "Puñao" a handful or "Puñaito" a little handful of whatever you want, dry pulses, nuts, fish, anything!

Incense to attract abundance and fortune

To make this incense we are going to need clean and dry fish bones, bay leaves, cinnamon, benzoin, amber or dry pine resin, nutmeg, galangal, basil, dried chamomile flowers, dried dandelion flowers and poppy seeds. We will proceed, grinding the fish bones and reserving them to the side. Then we will proceed grinding the rest of the spices and flowers. When they are ready we will add our pulverised fish bones to the mix and store in a dry place.

Incense for new beginnings

This is an incense that we can use to reinforce spells to promote new beginnings or to use as an offering if we are working with a deity for opening new paths.

To make this incense we will need snake bones, daffodil roots or flowers (I like dried flowers), lavender, rosemary, thyme, bay leaf, dried garlic, cloves, rose petals, red clover, pine needles, tobacco without additives, dragon's blood and myrrh. We will always start by grinding the snake bones. We reserve it in the mixing bowl and we will grind the rest of the ingredients according to the texture that we want to achieve and then we will mix everything in our bowl. Store in a dry place. If we are going to make incense cones, we can add a few drops of black pepper oil and distilled water to the mix while handling to make the cones or sticks.

Attraction incense

This is an incense that we can use alone or to reinforce spells to attract a person. We are going to need a pheasant bone or/

and a piece of deer antler, galangal, cinnamon, dried chillies, dragon's blood, rose petals, myrrh, cardamom, coriander, benzoin, saffron, rose water, dried figs and dates. Baking paper. We will grind the pheasant or/and even deer bone and put it in our mixing bowl. We will take the rest of the dry ingredients, that is, less the oils, the rose water and the fig. The reason why we leave the dried fig and dates aside is because they are sticky ingredients and we will use them to make a paste. We will grind the dry ingredients and put them in the bowl. Next, we will put the date, the dried fig, a little rose water and the oils in the stone mortar or blender to create a paste. When it is ready, we will add the ground bone to the mortar, and little by little we will add the rest of the ingredients that are already ground to our paste. We will mix well. When we are finished with the mixing, we will spread the paste on the baking paper, in a very thin layer, so that it dries quickly. You can put it to dry in the sun or put it in the oven at low temperature. So that it dries, but does not burn. While we remove it from the paper, we can make flakes to burn on top of charcoal. We could also make cones with the paste instead of using the oven paper, they will take longer to dry, that's all.

Protection incense

For this protective incense we need badger bone, even a small piece, sea urchin spines, limpets, valerian root, basil, laurel, dragon's blood, angelica root, fern (of any kind), sage, rosemary, cedar, anis and frankincense. A few drops of distilled water and a little honey.

We will grind the shells and bones until they are powder and we will reserve them in the mixing bowl. We will proceed to grind the herbs and resins and mix them with the bones. We will add the honey and a few drops of distilled water to make sticks or cones.

Incense for good luck

We can use this incense like the others, to enhance more complex spells or on its own, since we can use it when we need a push of good luck for something. We can burn it before going to an important meeting. To prepare this incense we will need: A piece of starfish (I find them dead on the shore, even if they are small, we can use them), deer antler, frankincense, dry moss, pine needles or pine resin or both, cinnamon, red clover, calendula flowers, ginger, lavender and dried peony flowers. Store in a dry place.

Chapter 3

Songs of the Bone Mother

The song of the Bone Mother is old. It doesn't contain specific words, it's more like a whisper, a humming. It is a song that can be accompanied with a drum, a rattle made of shells and bones. It is a primitive song that your bones and my bones recognize. Somehow this book is also a song. I'm trying to raise my voice to reclaim our bones and I hope that at this point you feel a little more connected to yours, also to your ancestors in some way, to our history as a species and everything that connects us. It's funny but when I started walking this Path of the Bones and La Huesera asked me to sing, I started writing songs and I even recorded some with horrible quality on my laptop, without a proper microphone, they are now kind of relics on my Youtube channel The Path of the Bones. Never mind the quality, I started to sing as she told me, I also sang to the people who came seeking healing in the rites, in the circles. Like La Huesera in Women who run with the Wolves, who sang to the wolf bones that she found on the mountain and brought them back to life. I believe that following the song of the Bone Mother helps us to reconnect with our bones, with our ancestors, with what we are at our core, somehow it also brings us back to life — it opens a new door of exploration of our being. The Bone Mother does not understand race, ethnicity, or skin colour, but she will read your bones like a newspaper! She sings to our bones beyond the flesh that covers them, she sings to all of us. No, she does not only live in remote primitive caves or gorges, she is stored in our cellular memory, in which we carry the DNA of the ancestors who venerated her, like that first Funerary Goddess and also Life Giver. In a way you already know her, she has been your invisible companion throughout this book-journey, as you turn every single page. Of course, it is your job, if you want to get closer to her and her teachings, get her out of these pages, take her to your reality, connect with her, honour her. Find her within yourself, working with your ancestors, also with the landscape that surrounds you, she is omnipresent.

Songs and Stories: Singing Bones and the Power of Fairy Tales

I remember going in the car with my father and how he told us stories, I remember my mother telling us stories when we were very little and I remember being in bed, snuggled up to my Great-grandmother, Fefa, while she told me stories on some cold February night in Jayena. I remember The Tale of Kiriko the Rooster, which my mother also told me and other stories. They are still there after all these years, in my head.

Folk tales have incredible power and many of them have survived for centuries. Andreas Johns gifted us with one of the best summaries of the core of fairytales that I have read, in his book *Baba Yaga the Ambiguous Mother and Witch of the Russian Folktale*:

> *In the guise of entertaining stories, the Indo-European fairy tale reflects concerns with the human condition: Life and death, sexual initiation, and old age (Belmont 1999: 211–212); the hero and heroine's journeys to and from "the other realm" are a denial of the irreversibility of real time and the inevitability of death. The passage of time is expressed in spatial terms as a journey to a symbolic "other world" or land of death. Unlike human beings, whose life journey proceeds in one direction only, the fairy tale heroine or hero can return from the other realm, reflecting the human desire to control time. This denial of time and death is the essential latent mythic content of the fairy tale.*

When I was a child, I was obsessed with a series of short books that recorded traditional tales from the oral culture in Spain, *Los Cuentos de la Media Lunita* (Tales of the Half Little Moon), compiled by Antonio Rodríguez Almodóvar, a writer born in Alcalá de Guadaira, Seville. The author became incredibly popular for his work by recovering these stories, many of them are centuries old and continue to be shared. The tale about Kiriko the Rooster is one of them.

We often find very dark elements in old stories. I vividly remember one of the stories in which a man kidnapped a little girl and put her in a sack, taking her from town to town hitting her with a stick to make her sing, and people gave him the money thinking it was a magic sack. Horrible, right? One of my favorite stories, La Flor de Lilila (The Lilila Flower), had very dark elements, it included a murder and singing bones.

We find elements in the Lilila Flower story in the famous tale by the Grimm Brothers, The Singing Bones. In this tale there are also three brothers and the older ones murder the youngest. The crime is discovered because someone makes a flute from the little brother's bones and the flute sings — telling the story of the crime. In another of their stories, The Story of the Youth Who Went Forth to Learn What Fear Was, they tell us in the adventure how some men played bowls with a skull and nine bones. In the Spanish History of the Flower, the fingers of the little brother's hand grow reeds with which the flute is made. Perhaps an attempt to soften the macabre charge of the story. This story also connects with another fairytale, The Twa Sisters, found sometimes under other names such as The Two Sisters or The Bonnie Swans, where the older sister also murders the younger one, and a magical instrument created from her body turned into reeds, will expose the crime. We also find in Perrault's story, Wonderful Birch, the bones of the victim — the mother of the heroine who is bewitched by a bad witch and turned into a black ram. She is later cooked and eaten by her husband and the witch. Her daughter would take her bones and bury them and they would turn into plants, in this case a birch tree. Of course, we don't only find bones in European fairy tales, there are stories related to bones in different cultures, we just need to search for them.

Bones Stories

In the Path of the Bones there are also stories. Sometimes they are visions, I have shared a couple already. Other times feelings that I transcribe become small stories. There are also traditional stories that I have adapted over time, because I have felt connected to them in some way or they spoke of Deities I worship.

She wolf (La loba/huesera)

This is a small excerpt that I wrote a few years ago. Sometimes I let my wounds bleed through my writing and I am not fully aware of the scope of my words. It happened with some other writings I shared in the past titled Amar a Una Sacerdotisa (To love a Priestess). Those excerpts that I wrote letting my soul bleed into words, ended up reaching thousands of people on Facebook and now they are waiting to be formatted in a small book that I have called the Invisible Sandals, about the path of the Priestess. She wolf has no destiny, but I think it expresses many things and that's what matters to me. And of course, it also contains bones!

There are those who will never see the She Wolf ... Those who knew her or who ever saw her will not be able to tell you too much about her. The She Wolf roams the woods, the mountain, and the river when there is no one nearby. The She Wolf is not a friend of the crowds, of being watched. For a long time she hid from those who roamed the forest and hunters.

She is the Shadow and Medicine ... She died. Yes, she died and the Great Spirit returned her to her body, brought her back into her broken bones. She almost went crazy with pain. The animals fled from her heartbreaking screams. The entire forest shook. She crawled to the river and dyed the waters with her blood. The icy waters slowly calmed her spirit.

She stopped crying. That day the Bear approached her and gave her fish and roots. When the Bear left, the Raven approached her and cleaned her wounds. Then came the Mountain Lion, who pulled her off the shore. He left her lying on the tall grass, under the sun so that her body got warm again.

The Raccoon approached her and disentangled her hair and the Squirrel brought her nuts. A Butterfly came to rest on her nose and tickle her and a Ladybug cleaned her ears. At dusk the Bear returned with more fish to lie beside her and give her warmth. Thus, for several days, the creatures of the forest, large and small, went to help the She Wolf and when she was able to get up she followed the Mountain Lion to the cave that would be her new home.

When she became strong, the She Wolf began to hunt for herself. Sometimes she found traps hidden in the forest and made them jump so that no animals were caught in them. She knew the evil of Man too well ... The forest was her home and its inhabitants her brothers. Sometimes she found dark traces of those that smell of pain and death ... She Wolf Medicine is powerful for many reasons. She has the Medicine of those who embraced Death, the Medicine of the Wound, also the Medicine that her Animal Brothers gave her. She covers herself with the black feathers of the Crow, forces you to look at the darkness that also shelters her.

If you heard her howl while wandering lost, if you crossed the Path of the She Wolf, don't fear. Maybe you had to find her or her to find you. The Great Spirit knows, Mother Earth knows, the Forest knows ... Your Soul knows ... Let the She Wolf tell you a story and sing to your bones. Her voice is also Medicine...

Sedna's story

Although it is very sad, I love the story of the Inuit Goddess Sedna. She also loses her fingers and they also transform, although not into trees. Last year I retold her story in my own way, using classical elements of the different versions for a conference. Re-telling this story, with all my respect, was a tribute to that drop of blood I carry from these people from the arctic.

Sedna was a very beautiful young woman, perhaps the most beautiful in the village. Her family was modest and her father hoped to marry her off well. He tried by all means for her to take a husband but she rejected all suitors who approached her, offending her father, as Sedna's fame for rejecting men began to spread, he was full of shame.

Rumours of Sedna's beauty travelled far from her village, so far that the King of the Fulmar became curious to meet her. With his magical powers, he transformed into a man and travelled to Sedna's town. Once there, he pretended not to know anything about her and did everything possible to meet her father. He introduced himself as an extraordinary hunter and told him that he came from a distant place where they lived very well off. Sedna's father, of course, thought that the hunter would be an ideal son-in-law and introduced him to Sedna. The hunter was captivated by her beauty and did everything possible to dazzle her but she was not fooled by him no matter how much the stranger promised her a luxurious life on the other side of the sea. Sedna's father, angry with his daughter for rejecting such a good match, played a trick on her in exchange for food that the hunter promised to bring him. Mischievously he gave Sedna a potion that made her sleep and so the hunter/King of Fulmar took her with him.

When Sedna woke up, she found herself in a huge bird's nest, surrounded by feathers and birds. She thought that the hunter had kidnapped her and asked for an explanation. To her surprise the hunter became the King of the Fulmar, a huge bird and told her that she now belonged to him and that she would have to live with him as his wife, which horrified Sedna. Several days passed, during the day the King of the Fulmar was a bird and hunted for Sedna and during the night he transformed into the hunter to lie with her.

Meanwhile Sedna's father in the village was still waiting for the food the hunter promised him but over time he realised that he had been deceived and became very angry. He went out to sea with his Kayak in search of the hunter and to bring back Sedna.

After several days he found her, sitting in the nest of the King of the Fulmar crying. She told him who the hunter really was and told her father that he was away fishing. Sedna's father realised that she didn't know that he had tricked her too but he didn't tell her anything about it and they set off in the kayak.

The King of the Fulmar returned to find the nest empty and went into a rage and flew until he found them. He flew over the kayak several times and flapped his wings so hard that he started raising a storm. Sedna's father was very scared and seeing that he was going to die he threw Sedna out of the Kayak, thinking that she would calm the King of the Fulmar. Horrified, Sedna grabbed onto the Kayak but her father cut her fingers off with his hunting knife. Sedna began to sink into the waters and as she descended, something changed.

So great was the injustice against her, so great the trauma suffered, so much her rage that her heart broke and as it did the sea water entered her heart and something wonderful happened. Marine animals and large mammals emerged from Sedna's fingers and Sedna herself was transformed by seawater and her human self died. Her heart began to shine with a bright blue light and the animals that had been born from her fingers surrounded her while a metamorphosis occurred. While she kept falling towards the bottom of the sea of ice and when she reached the bottom she would do it as a goddess of the depths, a Goddess of the underworld. A place where she would spend the rest of her days.

People say that while Sedna is calm there is good fishing and hunters can bring food home, but sometimes Sedna falls prey to memories and the betrayal and abuse still hurts. When this happens her very long hair becomes tangled and she traps the marine animals in it. When this happens there is no hunting and men go hungry. The shaman from the village has the job to travel to the ice underworld through dreams and convince Sedna that not all men are evil like her father.

It is not an easy task and sometimes a shaman has to go several times to calm her down and he combs her hair with a bone comb to free the trapped animals from the sea. Even now in our day, Sedna is the most important Goddess of the Arctic.

Baba Yaga and the Sun Child

We have already explored Baba Yaga in Chapter 4. I shared that she is closely related to bones and death. We will find references to bones and death in many Russian folk tales, but let me share with you a different story about Baba Yaga. This is an original story I wrote for another event that might help you understand another side of Baba Yaga, as I have experienced her.

Our history in this world clearly begins with our birth, but in my case, I will begin to tell my story from the moment my grandmother Yaga found me. It was cold, there was snow and a blizzard was blowing. Grandma told me that she had taken a lantern and that she had gone out to get wood for the fire with my aunty. Between the whistles of the blizzard, she heard something strange. Grandma has always had very sensitive hearing, I could say even supernatural, but of course, she is not a normal person. I think she never was. She told me how she followed what sounded like a small animal, but when she got closer, she realised it was a baby crying.

And she and my aunt found me, in the middle of that blizzard, barely wrapped in a blanket inside the trunk of a tree, freezing to death. A new born baby crying in despair. Grandma picked me up and wrapped me in her shawl and carried me in her arms, and they went back to her hut. When she pulled me out of my blanket she saw I was only a few hours old and that my umbilical cord had barely been tied.

Of course, Granma Yaga noticed something that made her understand why they had abandoned me like that. The mark that I bear on my chest, a huge birthmark that looks like a sun.

Grandma explained to me some years later that my parents were probably very superstitious and that when they saw that big mark, they became scared, thinking that somehow I was cursed or that it would bring them bad luck. Perhaps even fearing the reaction of the people in the village. But it would not be the first time that Yaga had found children in the forest. Some with some malformation. Sometimes she was too late and she found the tiny babies dead. She would then pick them up and take them to her house. There she performed a small ceremony for them and deposited them under her house, below the chimney, so that they would never be cold again. Those she found alive, she raised them like me and my aunty and when their time came they left her house and went to live in other villages, sometimes very far. But from time to time, my aunts would come to visit Yaga and bring her gifts. Sometimes they also came to ask for help. My grandmother Yaga was a wise woman, but you may already know this.

Yaga took care of me, as a mother would, together with my younger aunt, who helped Yaga. They bathed me by the fire and gave me goat's milk and oatmeal. I grew up healthy and happy and my hair turned golden like the rays of the sun. My other aunts came sometimes and played with me, when they weren't drying herbs or mushrooms. The truth is that Grandma was always very busy. Occasionally strangers came to seek her, but they rarely passed the door. A few times grandmother hid me in a large pot before they entered and so that I kept quiet she gave me bread and goat cheese.

One night Grandma Yaga woke me up. Several of my aunts had arrived. They had brought me new clothes and also boots and a coat that was too big for me. They all seemed very happy and gave me kisses. One put a crown made of pine on my head. Another gave me a copper bracelet. And so, in that manner, we left the Yaga's hut and began to walk, all following the grandmother. We came to a hill with some weird stones. Grandma told me they were very old, as old as her, and I looked at Yaga and shrugged. Grandma sat me down on one of the stones next to the food they had brought and my aunts began to dance and sing. The first rays of the morning sun bathed us and we saw how the sun rose in the east. When the sun was fully up, Grandma took off my coat and camisole, exposing my chest and birthmark. And she introduced me to the sun as his son, and she told the sun that I was old enough to receive a name and that since he was the God of Giving, they had brought me here for him to give me one. My youngest aunt left the circle to approach me. The sun father has spoken, she said, you will be named after a mountain, you will be called Kolovrat, Dimitri Kolovrat, the Sun Child. And all my aunts and grandmother Yaga shouted my new name. Between smiles and kisses, they dressed me and we walked back to Grandma's hut through the snow.

From that day on, that was my name. They never called me Sun Child anymore, as they had done until then, I became Dimitri. A few days after the ceremony, Grandma called me to her side near the fire and told me that when spring came, I was going to travel south with one of my aunts, that I was going to cross the mountains that bore my name and that I would have to leave offerings. I knew that my aunt lived in a city full of water, because sometimes she talked about her when she visited. She often brought nice fabrics for Yaga. She told me that I would have to learn a new language and go to school. That I had to study hard for her to be happy. She asked me to learn from the people, especially from those that came from far away, and that If I had the chance I shall travel, and see other places when I grew older, but I had to promise her to come back and tell her about what I saw.

When spring came, my aunt who lived in the city of water came for me and I said goodbye to Yaga like the child I was, crying and hugging my grandmother. In the village they were waiting for us with a carriage. We travelled for days and arrived at the place, my aunt told me that it was called Venice. My aunt did not live in a modest house, to my surprise my aunt lived in a big house with many rooms and there were more people living there, servants. She told me that when she was younger, she met her husband because he came to seek her help as he was sick. That she healed him and he asked her to marry him. Her husband was from a good family and over time, they moved to Venice for business, they had not had children, so when I moved in, I have to say, my uncle treated me well.

He played with me when he had time. He talked to me about business and ships and he used to take me to the port. I went to school and as I promised Grandma Yaga, I studied hard. My aunt travelled several times a year to see my grandmother, she brought herbs and medicines. My aunt used the teachings from Yaga, to work and help merchants and other people that felt sick. Sometimes in exchange for her help they would give her money, other times they reached a commercial agreement. My aunt was a very intelligent woman, but of course, Grandma Yaga had raised her!

The years passed and approaching my 16th birthday my aunt came to my room looking to talk to me. She told me that we were going to go on a trip to see Grandma Yaga, which made me very happy. Many years had passed but no matter how much I had learned in the city. Nothing made me forget Yaga. I also travelled a few times with my uncle and visited some countries in Europe, also the North of Africa. and somehow, I knew that she travelled with me.

We departed and after several days, we arrived at the village near the forest where the grandmother lived. There we left the car and continued on foot. Along the way I appreciated how my aunt was getting older and I couldn't help but wonder how Grandma Yaga was. Grandma's hut was there, although it seemed it had moved, but inside nothing had changed. Everything was still full of pots, herbs, bones and Grandma was sitting by the fire. Sun Child! she exclaimed and my heart skipped a beat. Yes grandma, it's me. I sat down next to her rocking chair, and she ruffled my blonde hair, and kissed my face and hands, and I held her close. How strange, it seemed to me that she was still the same as when I left while my aunt had aged. She got up and stood next to me, to see how tall I was. Gosh, I thought to myself, Grandma wasn't small, she was even taller than myself. And my aunt looked at us and smiled. And she began to ask me a *thousand and one things and I told her stories of my journeys, of the people, of the strange animals that I had seen in Africa. I spoke Italian, but also, I spoke some Latin, French and I wasn't bad in Spanish.*

Grandma Yaga's eyes shone with pride and I was happy to see her happy. She said loving words to my aunt, for giving me such a wonderful life and education. Grandma served us a bowl of soup and we went to rest from the trip. We spent several weeks with her, while she and my aunt worked preparing potions and other things, I also helped them a bit to collect the herbs in the wilds. I already knew the herbs, since I had helped grandma collect them many times as a child. My youngest aunt came to visit. She now lived in a village by the North Sea and had twin daughters who came with her. They were beautiful girls with red hair. My aunt's husband was a foreigner. All the years that had passed since I left for Venice until now, had disappeared and I felt like a child again, even my aunts seemed to get magically younger when they were close to grandma. As if time went backwards. I think we spent more than a month with Yaga, how beautiful were the summer days in the mountains. Grandmother told me that before I left I would have to go through a test and I agreed. I was to spend a whole day and a night in a special place, because I had to receive my fate.

I followed her through the woods, and we ended up at the hill with the stones where I got my name as a child. A few metres below, there was a large hole in the ground, like the mouth of a cave, but it was not a cave. The palace was huge and it was full of rocks, some of them with drawings. I also noticed human bones inside. "Dimitri, my Sun child. Let the rocks and bones speak to you. when you get a message return to the house or wait till I come". She said and left, leaving me only a few mushrooms to eat and a bit of water. I made my offering of food and honey water with milk and waited. My lantern illuminated the strange grotto. I found myself trying to guess what the drawings on the rock were and looking at the bones, wondering who they were. Then I remembered the mushrooms that my grandmother had left me.

169

She called these the Ears of the Invisible. I asked them to help me discover my future and I ate them.

And I gave thanks for my years with Grandma Yaga and I gave thanks for the love and for my luck, when she found me in the trunk of that tree. I thanked my aunts, who had given me so much love, for my uncle in Venice, thanks for the opportunity to have known other countries. I thanked those who were in this place, for receiving me. I was looking at my lantern but my eyes were closing. I started to hear songs, it's funny, because it sounded like my aunts singing. I opened my eyes and looked at the stones, a blue light began to shine, as if coming out of the drawings and between the lights I began to see some images, also the bones began to shine with the strange light, and the vision came. I saw myself crossing the sea in a ship to Constantinople. The bustling and rich city. But then I saw what looked like a battle, I saw several images of war, I saw myself, older, meeting with what seemed important people. The images became blurry and when they became clear again, I saw people leaving the city, which was left to be looted by the invaders. I closed my eyes for a while, but in my head, I kept seeing the images. I opened my eyes again and then I saw Grandmother Yaga. I saw how she said goodbye to one of my aunts and her cabin got up on her chicken feet and walked away into the forest, towards the Northeast. I also saw a young woman in bed, with dull eyes and blond hair, she seemed paralyzed. And I saw a very tall man walking away from her with a baby in his arms. Deep breath. I think I was seeing my parents. And I couldn't help but cry. The vision dissolved and I closed my eyes, trying not to see anything else and finally fell asleep. The rest of the time that I spent there I took it to meditate. When Grandma came back for me, she brought more water and some food. But she only offered me the water. She asked if I had seen my fate and I said yes. I shared with her my visions. I told her about the war, and she told me that I would have the ability to help some people when the time came. She also nodded when I told her that I saw her leave. To which she added that it was inevitable and that sometimes she travels far away. I shared the vision of my parents and she gave me a sad look and offered me something to eat. Back at the hut, Yaga told me to keep my visions and not to share them, except with my aunt if I wished to tell her. Although there were a few years for the vision to come true, she told me to keep learning and plan for the future. Some days passed and the time to leave came. When I said goodbye to Grandma she told me to write to her and also to my aunt and nieces on the North Coast, who sometimes complained that I had moved too far from her. That made me smile.

Years went by, I worked with my uncle, I met my wife and got married, and had children, prospering in life. I went back to visit Yaga several times over the years. The last time I travelled from Venice I took my eldest son with me, so that he could meet Grandma Yaga. And in all those years, she didn't change. We changed. When the time came for my aunt to die, she travelled to Yaga not to come back, just as my other aunts did. Also, the time of my visions also came and I was able to help a number of families to leave Constantinople, before the city fell. Unfortunately, not everyone listened to me, but I was able to help those who allowed themselves to be advised. Eventually I bought a house in Gdansk, not far from where my other aunt lived, looking for some peace and quiet; I left Venice to return to the North and settled there with my wife and children. And there I grew old, and when I found myself tired, I asked my eldest son to take me to Yaga. When we arrived, my grandmother's cabin was waiting for me in the usual place, with the smoke coming out the chimney. I said goodbye to my son Dimitri and continued to walk alone. The door opened and Grandma Yaga came out to the door to wait for me with a smile.

Songs from the Path of the Bones

When La Huesera asked me to sing as part of the healing work of the Path of the Bones, I composed several medicine songs. Some celebrate the menstruating woman, others the wise woman, others the healer that every woman carries inside, another celebrates love, others maternity and thus a complete list of original and healing songs for significant moments in our lives.

Some of them mention bones so here they are. Although the original lyrics were in Spanish, I have translated and arranged them so that they retain their rhythm and power when sung.

She Wolf Song (Loba)

ah ooouuu (howling)
ah ooouuu
ah ooouuu
Ah ah ooouuu...
Loba, smell the Blood
Of my Wounds.
Loba, find the Shadows
at the gorge.
Loba, lick the salt
off my Cheeks.
Loba, under the moon
I heal and I howl with you...
ah ooouuu
ah ooouuu
ah ooouuu
Ah ah ooouuu...
Loba, I'm biting the stars
Of my night.
Loba, I'm freeing my soul
from its hooks.
Loba, I'm running wild
In the mountains.
Loba, that under the moon
I heal and I howl with you...
ah ooouuu
ah ooouuu
ah ooouuu
Ah ah ooouuu...
Loba, find the bones

Of other Women.
Loba, I'm weaving
Lives with my Teeth.
Loba, I'm finding the light
In my entrails.
Loba, under the moon
I heal and I howl with you...
ah ooouuu
ah ooouuu
ah ooouuu
Ah ah ooouuu...

The Song of the Blood
As a Sacred Woman
I sing to my Blood,
As a Sacred Woman
I sing to my Bones,
As a Sacred Woman
I sing to my path,
I sing my path
Under the cloak of the Moon.
Eh ya eh ya ya eh ya he
Eh ya eh ya ya eh ya oh
As a Sacred Woman
I sing to my fire
as a Sacred woman
I sing to my Womb,
As a Sacred Woman
I sing my path
I sing my path
Under the cloak of the Moon.
Eh ya eh ya ya eh ya he
Eh ya eh ya ya eh ya oh

Ancestors Song
I wanna pray to my blood
I wanna pray to my bones
Honouring those who departed,
Today I call those who were.
I come to look for the medicine
I come to search in the shadows
I wish to bring sun and stars,
I wish to heal the wounds.
I sing to the love in my bones
I sing to love in their souls
I wish to heal the wrongs,
I wish to free the chain.
I live in my ancestors
I live because you were here
I wear your skin on my skin,
I bring light to my blood…

Bibliography and References

Abram, C. 2006. *Viking and Medieval Scandinavia Vol. 2. Hel in Early Norse Poetry*. Brepols.

Aeschylus. 2012. *Prometheus Bound*. Translated by Ian Johnston Vancouver Island University.

Afanas'ev, Aleksandr. 1945. *Russian Fairy Tales*. Translated by Norbert Guterman. The Pantheon Fairy Tale & Folklore Library.

A Hymn to Bau's Beneficent Protective Goddess. The Electronic Text Corpus of Sumerian Literature. University of Oxford.

Bakilan, F, Zelveci D. D. 2020. *Musculoskeletal problems during pregnancy*. J Clin Med Kaz.

Beeman, William O. 2015. *Religion and Ritual Performance.* La cronoyance et le corps. Esthétique, corporéité et identités. Pag. 35–58. Universite de Bordeaux.

Bidwell, P. 2008. *The History of Native American Bone Chokers*. (Article)

Bonfante, L. 2016. *Human sacrifices and taboos in antiquity: notes on an Etruscan funerary urn*.

Borg-Cardona, A. 2013. 'The Marine Shell in and around the Maltese Islands'. *The Galpin Society Journal Vol. 66*.

Brinton, D.G. 1890. 'Folk-Lore of the Bones'. *The Journal of American Folklore*.

Carriço, H. M. 2018. *Scrimshaw — A arte dos baleeiros nos Açores. um património a conhecer a defender e salvaguardar*. Universidade de Lisboa.

Clottes, J. and Lewis-Williams, D. 1996. *Los Chamanes de la Prehistoria*. Editorial Ariel.

Cooper, B. 1997. 'Baba-Yaga, the Bony-Legged: A Short Note on the Witch and Her Name'. *New Zealand Slavonic Journal*.

C. G. Wagner. 2019. Algunas consideraciones sobre los rituales de Astarté. Una aproximación etnobotánica. La vie, la mort et la religión dans l'universe phénicien et punique. VIIème congrès international des études phéniciennes et puniques. Institut National du Patrimoine.

d'Este, S., Rankine, D. 2009, *Visions of the Cailleach: Exploring the Myths, Folklore and Legends of the pre-eminent Celtic Hag Goddess*. Avalonia Books.

Edmonds III, R. G. 2019. *Drawing Down the Moon: Magic in the Ancient Greco-Roman World*. Princeton University Press.

Edrey M, 2008. *The Dog Burials at Achaemenid Ashkelon Revisited*. Tel Aviv, 35:2,267–282, DOI:10.1179/tav.2008.2008.2267

Ellis, B. 2002 *Why Is a Lucky Rabbit's Foot Lucky? Body Parts as Fetishes*. Journal of Folklore Research Vol. 39, No. 1, pp 51–84. Indiana University Press.

Flad, R. K. 2008. *Divination and Power: A Multiregional View of the Development of Oracle Bone Divination in Early China. Current Anthropology, Vol 49, pp 403–437. The University of Chicago Press.* .

Frazer, J. G. 1937. *The Object of Head-Hunting*. The Rengma Nagas. Macmillan and Co.

Garcia de la Cuesta, D. 2019. *Acercamiento a la Mari Lwyd, Caballos, Gumias, Cabras, Toros, Vacas y Tzamálas en las Mascaradas*.

Germonpré ,M., Hämäläinen, R. 2007. *Fossil Bear Bones in the Belgian Upper Paleolithic: The Possibility of a Proto Bear-Ceremonialism*. Artic Anthropology,Vol 44. pp 1–30. University of Wisconsin Press.

Gonzalez Wagner, C. 2022. *Las Drogas Sagradas de la Antigüedad*. Alianza Editorial.

Graf, Fritz. *Magic in the Ancient World*. Harvard University Press, 2003.

Gregorie, S. 2011. 'Orígenes de la ocupación humana de Europa: Guadix-Baza y Orce, Menga. *Journal of Andalucian Prehistory, vol 2*.

Guzón Nestar, J. L. 2012. *Atapuerca y la Evolución Humana* (Article).

Harrington, N. 2015. *Ancestors and Ancestor Worship* for Vocabulary for the Study of Religion. Volume 1. Brill.

Hazzard-Donald, K. 2013. *Mojo Working: The old African American Hoodoo System.* University of Illinois Press.

Hodgkins, J., Orr, C. M., Gravel-Miguel, C. et al. 'An infant burial from Arma Veirana in northwestern Italy provides insights into funerary practices and female personhood in early *Mesolithic Europe. Sci Rep 11, 23735 (2021)'..*

Hurston, Z. (1931). 'Hoodoo in America'. *The Journal of American Folklore.*

Ivantis, L. J. 1992. *Russian Folk Belief.* M.E. Sharpe.

Johns A. 2004. *Baba Yaga the Ambiguous Mother and witch of the Russian Folktale.*

Kapcár, A. 2015. *The Origins of Necromancy or How We Learned to Speak to the Dead.*

Kenney, E., & Gilday, E. T. 2000. 'Mortuary Rites in Japan: Editors' Introduction'. *Japanese Journal of Religious Studies, 27(3/4).*

Kovacs, C.S. 'Calcium and Bone Metabolism in Pregnancy and Lactation'. *The Journal of Clinical Endocrinology & Metabolism, Volume 86, Issue 6, 1 June 2001.*

Laufer, B. 1923. *Use of Human Skulls and Bones in Tibet.*

Leeming, D. 2005. *The Oxford Companion to World Mythology.* Oxford University Press.

Lopez Ruiz, C. 2022. *Phoenicians and the Making of the Mediterranean.* Harvard University Press.

Lowe, J. E. 1929 *Magic in Greek & Latin Literature.* Blackwell — Oxford.

Luck, G. 1987. *Arcana Mundi: Magic and the Occult in the Greek and Roman Worlds: A Collection of Ancient Texts.* Crucible.

Manologas, S. Birth and Death of the Bone Cells. 'Endocrine Reviews', Volume 21, Issue 2, 1 April 2000.

McAleese, K. 1998. 'The reinterment of Thule Inuit burials and associated artefacts' — *IdCr-14 Rose Island, Saglek Bay, Labrador. Études/Inuit/Studies, 22(2)*.

McCormick, J. P. and Parascandola J. 1981. Dragon Bones and Drugstores. Pharmacy and History, Vol 23, No 2, pp 55–70. The University of Wisconsin..

Museo Arqueologico y Etnologico Provincial. 1994. Rituales Funerarios en la Provincia de Granada (Arqueología de la Muerte).

Mylona, D. 2013. *Dealing with the unexpected. Unusual animals in an Early Roman cistern fill in the Sanctuary of Poseidon at Kalaureia, Poros*. Bones, behaviour and belief. Svenska Institutet I Athens Monographs.

Nagy, M. 1991. *Bone and Antler Tools from a Late Prehistoric Mackenzie Inuit Site*. Association Canadienne D'Archéologie Cahier No. 1

Nagy, M. 2018. 'Reinterpreting the First Human Occupations of Ivujivik (Nunavik, Canada)'. *Arctic Anthropology, 55(2)*.

Nifosi, A. 2021. (Conference) *Astragalomaniacs: Knucklebones in the Ancient World Manchester Games Studies*.

Ogden, D. 2004. *Greek and Roman Necromancy*. Princeton University Press.

Ogden, D. 2009. *Magic, Witchcraft and Ghosts in the Greek and Roman Worlds*. Oxford University Press.

Ogden, D. 2008. *Night Black Agents. Witches, Wizards and the Dead in the Ancient World*. Hambledon Continuum.

Ojo, O. 2004. 'Slavery and Human Sacrifice in Yorubaland'. *Journal of African History*. .

Parker Pearson, M. 1999. *The Archeology of Death and Burial Sutton Publishing Limited*.

Pinkola Estes, Clarissa. 1992. *Women Who Run with the Wolves: Contacting the Power of the Wild Woman*. Rider & Co.

Ragot, N. 2009. 'Ritos Y Rituales En Torno A Mictlantecuhtli. Image and Ritual in the Aztec World (*Acte du IIème Congrès International de la Société Américaniste de Belgique, Louvain-la-Neuve*).

Rainio, R. and Tamboe, A. 2018. Animal Teeth in a Late Mesolithic Woman's Grave, Reconstructed as a Rattling Ornament on a Baby Pouch. EXARC Journal. Issue 2018/1.

Rankine, D. 2022. *The Grimoire Encyclopaedia*. West Yorkshire: Hadean Press.

Rawlinson, G. 1909. *The History of Herodotus*. Tandy-Thomas, New york.

Rowe, M. 2003. 'Grave Changes: Scattering Ashes in Contemporary Japan'. *Japanese Journal of Religious Studies, 30(1/2)*.

Sakashita, Jay. 'Cremation And Death Rituals'." *MidWeek*.2 July 2014

Serrano Sanchez, C. 2010, Medicina tradicional y la medicina basada en la evidencia. El caso de un huesero de dos comunidades afromestizas de Veracruz, México. Anales de Antropologia, Vol. 42. Instituto de Investigaciones Antropologicas. UNAM. (Universidad Nacional Autonoma de Mexico).

Stenton, D.R. 1991.*The adaptive significance of caribou winter clothing for arctic hunter-gatherer. Études Inuit Studies. Vol. 15. No 1. Adaptation, Ethnohistoire, Langue/Adaptation, Ethnohistory and Language. Pp. 3–28. University Laval.*

Svanberg, I. *Central Asiatic Journal Vol. 31, No. 1/2 (1987)* 'The Folklore of Teeth Among Turkic and Adjacent Peoples'.

Syro-Mesopotamian Studies. The Oriental Institute Oxford University.

Taylor, R. RES: Anthropology and Aesthetics No. 48, Autumn, 2005. Roman Oscilla: An Assessment. The University of Chicago Press.

The Oxford Handbook of the Archaeology of Ritual and Religion. 2011. OUP.

Thomas Hutcheson, C. 2022. *New World Witchery.* Llewellyn.

Thoms, William J. 'Divination by the Blade-Bone.' *The Folk-Lore Record, vol. 1, 1878, pp. 176–79.*

Wells, P. J. 2018. 'Some Unique Bone, Antler and Ivory Artefacts from Phillip's Garden (EeBi-1), a Dorset Paleo-Inuit Settlement in Northwestern Newfoundland'. *Arctic, 71(3).*

Wygnańska, Z. *Equid and Dog burials in Syria and Mesopotamia.* 2017. Aram Society for Wagner.

www.atlasobscura.com

www.cailleachs-herbarium.com

www.catacombepalermo.it

www.dbe.rah.es

www.livescience.com

www.mesagrandeband-nsn.gov

www.nativeground.com

www.neandertals.org

www.inuitsculptures.com

www.ukfossils.co.uk

www.viajesalaprehistoria.com

Bestsellers from Moon Books

Keeping Her Keys
An Introduction to Hekate's Modern Witchcraft
Cyndi Brannen
*Blending Hekate, witchcraft and personal development together
to create a powerful new magickal perspective.*
Paperback: 978-1-78904-075-3 ebook 978-1-78904-076-0

Journey to the Dark Goddess
How to Return to Your Soul
Jane Meredith
*Discover the powerful secrets of the Dark Goddess and transform
your depression, grief and pain into healing and integration.*
Paperback: 978-1-84694-677-6 ebook: 978-1-78099-223-5

Shamanic Reiki
Expanded Ways of Working with Universal Life Force Energy
Llyn Roberts, Robert Levy
*Shamanism and Reiki are each powerful ways of healing; together,
their power multiplies. Shamanic Reiki introduces techniques to
help healers and Reiki practitioners tap ancient healing wisdom.*
Paperback: 978-1-84694-037-8 ebook: 978-1-84694-650-9

Southern Cunning
Folkloric Witchcraft in the American South
Aaron Oberon
*Modern witchcraft with a Southern flair, this book is a journey
through the folklore of the American South and a look at the power
these stories hold for modern witches.*
Paperback: 978-1-78904-196-5 ebook: 978-1-78904-197-2

Readers of ebooks can buy or view any of these bestsellers by clicking on the live link in the title. Most titles are published in paperback and as an ebook. Paperbacks are available in traditional bookshops. Both print and ebook formats are available online.

Find more titles and sign up to our readers' newsletter
http://www.johnhuntpublishing.com/paganism

For video content, author interviews and more, please subscribe to our YouTube channel.

MoonBooksPublishing

Follow us on social media for book news, promotions and more:

Facebook: Moon Books Publishing

Instagram: @moonbooksjhp

Twitter: @MoonBooksJHP

Tik Tok: @moonbooksjhp